TWO HOUSES

AUP Titles of Related Interest

TWO HOUSES
New Tarbat, Easter Ross
Royston House, Edinburgh

MONICA CLOUGH

'I secured him and his heirs in ... two dwelling houses fully furnished, better than any other in the North of Scotland.'
George first Earl of Cromartie, 1707

ABERDEEN UNIVERSITY PRESS
Member of Maxwell Macmillan Pergamon Publishing Corporation

First published 1990
Aberdeen University Press

© Monica Clough 1990

British Library Cataloguing in Publication Data

Clough, Monica
  Two houses: New Tarbat House, Easter Ross,
  Royston House, Edinburgh, and the family of
  Mackenzie, Earls of Cromartie, 1656–1784
  1. Scotland, Highland Region. Cromarty. County
  Estates: Cromartie Estate, history
  I. Title
  941.172

ISBN 0 08 040909 1

Typeset and printed by AUP Glasgow/Aberdeen—a member of BPCC Ltd.

In memory of
EARL RORIE
Seventh Earl of Cromartie
1904–1989

Contents

List of Illustrations

List of Maps

Acknowledgements

My chief debt is to Roderick, seventh Earl of Cromartie for the generous way in which he unreservedly threw open his collection of papers. He also gave me the benefit of his own oral traditions of his family estate. This book is entirely based on these papers, now deposited on loan in the Scottish Record Office, Edinburgh. I am equally grateful to Lilias Countess of Cromartie who encouraged my constant visits to the Castle and helped the researcher in every way. I am grateful also to John, eighth Earl of Cromartie; and to my former tutor and collaborator Eric Richards, who taught me the questions to ask, and for the encouragement and tolerance of my family. Dr Frances Shaw in particular among the staff of the Scottish Record Office must be thanked. The Duke of Buccleuch kindly gave permission to use two maps of Royston in his possession, which Jane Watson re-drew. Ian Reid took photographs. Isabel Miller translated much of my handwriting into typescript. Jane Durham, David Alston, Catriona MacDonald, Alasdair Cameron, Geoffrey Jenkinson and Annette Hope have all been generous with information from their own fields of interest. The interpretations I have placed on all this information are, however, entirely my own.

Monica Clough
Milton
Glen Urquhart
Inverness

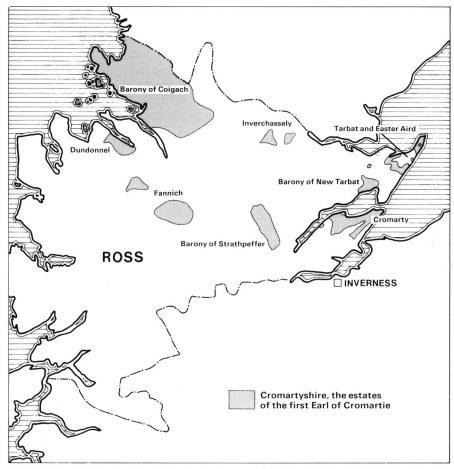

Map 1   General outline of Ross.

Introduction

In a sense this is a scrap-book of the affairs of two great houses, Tarbat in Ross-shire and Royston in Edinburgh. For five years I read the family papers which had accumulated for three centuries in the possession of the Earls of Cromartie at Castle Leod in Ross. Some were immaculately listed. Some were in the Estate Office, or its loft. Some were under the billiard table. Four great safes, of Great Exhibition model, held bundles of letters and the Charters. Drawers and bureaux disclosed more letters. Many were bound up in 23 big books in legal categories chosen by William Fraser who, a hundred years before, had printed two volumes based on what he considered the most interesting documents; interesting then, but we have a different kind of curiosity now. Fraser chronicled exchanges with other great nobles of the day, and meticulously recorded the stages by which the family of Sir Rory Mackenzie—brother to Mackenzie of Kintail the Chief and Tutor to his young son—had, in the early seventeenth century, acquired lands, prestige and titles second only to Seaforth himself. No breath of comment or criticism was recorded by Fraser.

Today historians are especially interested in social and economic history, and particularly, so far as owners of great Highland estates are concerned, in the relationships between landlord and tenant, also in the internal pressures generated by the conduct of the owners themselves, and in the external pressures of politics, warfare and changing economic circumstances.

How responsible were the owners of vast Highland estates for the great changes which occurred during the eighteenth and nineteenth centuries? Can any pattern be discerned and how typical was the experience of the Cromartie Estates? Based on a detailed study of the Cromartie Papers, these are the questions to which Eric Richards and I addressed ourselves in *Cromartie: Highland Life 1650–1914* (Aberdeen University Press, 1989). William Fraser's *The History of the Earls of Cromartie* 1877, is still available for the student of families and of genealogy. Earl Rorie wrote, while a prisoner of the Germans between 1940 and 1945, the admirable *A Highland History*, published in 1979.

None of these volumes really gives much sense of the life led in the houses owned by the family, nor of the personalities and peculiarities of the Mackenzies of Cromartie, nor their relations, neighbours, and servants. Glimpses which illuminate their times abound in the Cromartie Papers. Did it matter that George Mackenzie of Tarbat, the first earl, never travelled without a small copper coffee-pot, which is inventoried from 1678, when he was occupying an apartment in the Palace of Holyrood, till the day he died in 1714? He must have had chilly feet, as a pair of swansdown slippers also accompanied him for years. When he became an old man, retired from the rigours of his political career, he became an obsessional maker of lists, including one of 'The Stockings in my Chist'— inevitably some of the stockings were odd ones. This book was nearly called 'The Stockings in the Chist', as it is a collection of scraps from the Cromartie Papers which I find interesting and revealing. The scraps refer to the two main houses: New Tarbat in Easter Ross, and Royston in Edinburgh.

For detailed accounts of the family and the Estate the reader may refer to the other books quoted, and to the shortened table of genealogy. A brief outline of the family history follows, in an attempt to put the family into their context in Ross-shire and in the world outside, in the Edinburgh of the Restoration, and as visitors to Whitehall and Kensington Palace, the seats of power. The period covered is roughly the century from 1680 to 1780; both before and after these dates, surviving personal documents happen to be much more rare. The spellings of the originals have usually been retained, and a glossary will be found at the end of the book. It should be remembered that the Scots currency was severely devalued against the English currency, standing (for nearly all the period covered in these pages) at twelve pounds Scots to one pound sterling.

I

The People of the Houses

Family Portraits

The family of Mackenzie of Tarbat, later Earls of Cromartie, owed its high position in the strictly patriarchal Highland society to the fact that Sir Rory Mackenzie was a son of the clan chief. After the death of Kenneth, his elder brother, in 1611, Sir Rory became Tutor (Guardian) to his young nephew the new Chief and served (as his father and grandfather had done) as right hand of the Stuart Kings of Scotland in the North West. The Highlands were just coming out of a period of feuding and aggrandisment which established some families firmly, while others began to decline as central govenment strengthened. The scene in Ross was particularly complicated by the earlier extinction of the royal line of the Earls of Ross, and of the Lordship of the Isles. Royal patronage promoted Clan Mackenzie into many of the lands and positions formerly filled by the Earls and Lords of the Isles, and after the break with the Church of Rome in 1560 the Mackenzies were rewarded with the lands and dues that had formerly belonged to the Bishop of Ross. In return they served the Crown loyally for generations. Sir Rory's great-grandfather, John of Killin, was not the first of his family to come from Wester Ross to Easter Ross, but he was the first to acquire Castle Leod and the crannog fort of Kinellan. John fought at Flodden, and is credited with planting two Spanish chest-nuts in the park of Castle Leod to mark the confirmation of Saisin of Castle Leod by Mary Queen of Scots, at Inverness on 19 July 1556, trees which still flourish. He died aged eighty in 1561, having fought at Flodden at the King's right hand.

Sir Rory added to the Castle Leod property by purchasing the lands of Tarbat in Easter Ross in 1623. He had married an heiress, Dame Margaret MacLeod of Lewis, as part of a pacification of the west undertaken for the

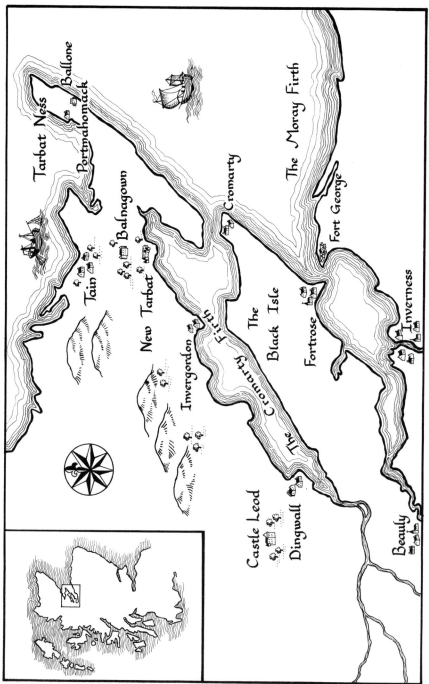

Map 2   New Tarbat and Easter Ross, redrawn from Avery's Map of Moray, 1727, by Janet Watson.

King which included the conclusion of a furious private feud between the MacLeods and Mackenzies. Dame Margaret brought him the Barony of Coigach in 1606, which extended over most of the northern shores of Loch Broom in Wester Ross. Perhaps as a compromise between the cornlands and Pictish remains of Tarbat in the east and the pastoral wilderness of Coigach in the west Sir Rory and his wife made their home at Castle Leod in the heartland, the Barony of Strathpeffer in mid Ross-shire where they extended the old castle and rebuilt its principal rooms and entrance: Castle Leod still has their initials, coat of arms and the date of their marriage, 1606, over the renaissance doorway, and on the topmost gable the date of completion, 1616. Sir Rory extended the family lands by purchase as well as by marriage, and at his death his family owned most of the Tarbat peninsula, known then as the Barony of Easter Aird, and, then as now, excellent corn land.

His son Sir John was a quieter man, he married the Lady Margaret Erskine, took a modest part in local affairs, and when civil war loomed, signed the Solemn League and Covenant. Most of the nobility of Scotland had done the same. He sat, representing Ross, in the famous Synod of Glasgow which rejected the King's authority in things spiritual. The fortunes of the Civil War swept up and down Scotland, and eventually Sir John became sickened by the pious excesses of the ayatollahs of the Covenanting party and joined the King's party. It is not certain what he was doing at the time of Montrose's last campaign in the Highlands; Sir John was a sick man at the time. There would have been much stir at the news of Montrose's defeat at Carbisdale and betrayal at Assynt at the hands of a distant Tarbat connection Macleod of Assynt—or was it at the hands of his dominating wife, Jean Munro of the family of Foulis? At any rate Sir John rallied after the execution of King Charles I, enough to join the Remonstrancers and the Scottish army that went south in a vain bid to restore King Charles II. He took his eldest son, George, then aged about eighteen, with him to Worcester and to fight in the battle which Cromwell won so easily. Charles hid in the oak tree, and the Scottish army was dispersed. Sir John came home to die in 1654, in Ballone in Tarbat.

George began his long career in the service of the house of Stuart as an exile. He was then involved in the Glencairn Rising, when a number of Scottish Highland nobility took arms against the Commonwealth and the rule of the New Model Army, represented by Col Lilburne and Col Monck in Scotland. King Charles II's commander, General Middleton, landed at Tarbat from Holland, and George was one of his officers. Glencairn's Rising was in essence the prototype of the next hundred years of Jacobite risings, down to the protagonists whose grandsons fought at Culloden, and to the perennial problems of lack of support, and promises unkept of gold and arms to be shipped from France. After Monck restored order George went into hiding, 'skulking' (the contemporary word for it), in the Western Isles with Sir Robert Moray. Subsequently they were heard of on the continent together. Moray also survived to become an ornament of the returned King Charles's court, and the first Secretary of the Royal Society of which George was a founder member. What Sir George did on the continent is uncertain, somewhere he acquired a good knowledge of French and the law, and the courtly manners for which he was renowned. It is more likely that these were the products of a sojourn in Europe than of his spell at Aberdeen University, when he had graduated at the usual age of fifteen. He had married in 1654 just before his father's death. His bride was Anne Sinclair of Mey and their marriage lasted forty-three years.

The year 1660 saw King Charles II on his throne and Sir George back in Edinburgh, as lieutenant to General Middleton, now King's Commissioner for Scotland. He was bidding for a political career. His first essay in this was disastrous, and lost him royal favour for many years. Though on the whole the return of the King was greeted with approval in Scotland, and the country settled to acquiescent peace, there were many scars left by the Civil War, particularly on the religious bodies in the country. Sir George Mackenzie of Tarbat, as he was generally known, an episcopalian and 'furious cavalier' tried to exclude those of presbyterian affiliations from the government of the day, in an intrigue known as The Balloting Affair. As the King leaned on the goodwill and ability of Lauderdale and his presbyterian friends for keeping Scotland peaceful and content, Tarbat's intervention was crass and inept and he was stripped of his recently acquired office as a Lord of Session. He did not recover royal favour until 1674 although he remained as a Lord in Parliament. He spent nearly twelve years in the north, laying the foundation of the much bigger estates he was to leave his sons. Unfortunately there is not much surviving correspondence in the family papers from this period. His return to royal favour was apparently helped by his kinsman, Sir George Mackenzie of Rosehaugh, Lord Advocate and his brother Roderick who, though a bit of a rogue, had married the daughter of Archbishop Burnet. As Lauderdale's health began to fail, Tarbat was amongst the coming men. He was then about forty, thought to be a bit old for a new start. However he rose rapidly, to become a Privy Councillor, Lord of Session and Lord Register Clerk of Scotland, under James VII and II; trusted advisor to the Crown under William and Mary, and Secretary of State under Queen Anne. He was an ardent advocate of the Union of Parliaments, which took place in 1707 after much campaigning. He died in 1714 aged eighty-two, on hearing of the death of Queen Anne and that the English magnates had sent for the Elector of Hanover. His political career has not had the recognition that it maybe deserves, but neither this volume nor an estate history is the place for it. He had an agile mind and a reputation for being slippery, and was involved in at least two accusations of malfeasance and peculation, from which he emerged buoyantly. He also was famous for great charm of manner, a facet which comes over as clearly in his correspondence as do his wily characteristics. Whatever may be said about his 'maggoty schemes' and his untrustworthiness (and plenty was said by his opponents, and by presbyterian historians thereafter) he remained at the centre of state affairs, constant to the House of Stuart and to the unpopular tenets of the episcopalian church of Scotland. His memory has sometimes suffered from a popular confusion with his cousin and contemporary Sir George Mackenzie of Rosehaugh, nicknamed 'The Bloody Mackenzie' for his supposed part in putting down the Covenanting insurrection of 1674. George Mackenzie of Tarbat was not Bloody—he was certainly wily.

During his sojourn out of favour in Ross at the beginning of the Restoration Tarbat looked about for means of making money. The grain export trade of the Moray coastal farms was already highly organised, with the main crop of bere barley. Bere was the staple of the whole of seventeenth century Scotland, consumed as baked barley bannock or brewed into beer or distilled into whisky. Oats were considered a luxury, more difficult to grow, in Stuart times. All Tarbat's and his neighbours' rents were paid in measures of bere barley and there was usually a considerable surplus. In his grandfather's day the Burgh of Tain exported bere by the shipload to Bergen in Norway, and Tarbat inherited a routine, which he greatly expanded, for shipping grain from his own lands to the merchants and brewers of Edinburgh and also the surplus from his neighbours' harvests which he had purchased. All the rents of the Baronies of Tarbat, Easter Aird and Strathpeffer were paid in kind, by the boll measure of bere barley. The tenants were also bound to 'lead the rent', that is to convey the grain to whichever girnel the lord designated. Charter parties were made in March of each year with a reliable skipper of a vessel in the coastal trade, to call in May at one of the little ports of the area for 'a fully lading' of grain, which was then sold under contract to a merchant brewer in Leith or Edinburgh. This was the main source of cash income from the estate. Tarbat set about improving the turnover.

Shipping was one of the keys to progress, and he embarked on some ambitious capital schemes to expedite his grain trade. At Portmahomack in the parish of Tarbat he built a girnel house for storage and a new harbour whose walls were extended by Thomas Telford 150 years later, and both still stand. Portmahomack was at the extreme easterly end of his properties; other ships plied on his business to Dingwall and to the Sands of Nigg, by the ruined Munro castle which became his mansion of New Tarbat. By far the best anchorage in the Firth of Cromarty was at

2　Anna Sinclair, Lady Tarbat, wife of the first Earl, who died in 1699.

1　George, Lord Tarbat, painted about 1690.

the town of Cromarty, a Royal Burgh set in the lands of the Urquhart Laird of Cromarty, with good arable land and a good harbour. Tarbat with his cousin Rosehaugh and a friend from Moray shore, Brodie of Leithen, and another Moray laird, Sir Thomas Calder, formed a consortium to acquire the lands of Cromarty. These lands were very ancient and included a small Sheriffdom dating back to the early middle ages; the Urquhart family had by the 1670s fallen on evil days since the scholarly old Sir Thomas, writer and translator of Rabelais, and fellow fighter for the King at the Battle of Worcester had 'died of laughter' in France on hearing of King Charles' restoration to the throne in 1660.

The partners started lending money to the extravagant young Urquharts who in turn inherited until their 'craizied estate' was entirely in Bond to one or other of the consortium. In the end Tarbat who had been created a Viscount by James VII and II was able to buy out the share of Brodie, who had acquired the Burgh; Rosehaugh took some of the good farms such as Navity which marched with his own lands, and Calder also sold out, taking the rights to the salmon fishing of Conon on lease from Tarbat. The last of the Urquharts of that branch went to be a soldier in the Low Country, with his uniform and commission bought by Tarbat.

Tarbat now controlled the best harbour on the north side of the Moray Firth and he had his own Sheriffdom. When a few years later Queen Anne made him an earl he took his title from Cromarty, (adopting the spelling of Cromartie) and all his other lands were included in what became the curious hybrid county of Ross-and-Cromarty as a Regality. This lasted as the separate entity of 'Cromartyshire' in fourteen enclaves within Ross until reabsorbed in late Victorian times. To have the Heritable Jurisdiction of your own lands and be judge in all the cases (bar treason) which affected your own tenantry was an advantage that major Scottish landowners were only to lose after the battle of Culloden in 1746.

To be a political figure in Scotland in the late seventeenth century it was necessary to look the part—to own a great mansion-house. At least one. In order to take a leading part in the politics of the day it was also necessary to have a town house in Edinburgh. George, the first earl, was a great builder. Early in his career he set about rebuilding near the site of the Munro castle of Milton, in Ross. This he called New Tarbat, moving the centre of his family holdings from the distant peninsula of Tarbat. New Tarbat became magnificent. Castle Leod, his favourite home in mid Ross, had been rebuilt by his grandfather, and the first earl did not alter it though he replaced the thatch with slates. His chief endeavours were at New Tarbat and at Royston in Granton, Edinburgh. The Edinburgh house still stands in the shadow of the city gas-holders. It was renamed Caroline Park by a later owner, and a description by John Gifford may be found in the Penguin *Guide to Edinburgh* (1986).

With the help of the Inventars of Royston we may get some idea of the house which was built and furnished by Tarbat in modest but direct emulation of Lord Lauderdale's Ham House in Richmond. We also get some idea of the cost of keeping up the style demanded of a Lord in the public eye, let alone in the Royal eye. It was all too expensive to be supported on the fragile grain trade of Easter Ross and such salaries, pensions and other fees as undoubtedly came the way of influential Officers of State. Both King James and King William gave Tarbat a pension of £400 sterling per annum; Queen Anne's intended generosity was never actually paid, according to the Earl, only promised. There is never a moment when one can draw up an accurate balance sheet for the first Earl; his finances were too involved. There was a network of Bonding and lending between members of the family, including Tarbat's large share in Seaforth's debt to the Crown, and in the money he and his sons owed the merchants of Edinburgh for money lent and goods supplied. The first Earl was the father of an expensive family. His four daughters were apparently well-married: to Bruce of Clackmannan, Brown of Coalston, Stewart of Balcaskie and a Sinclair cousin, a son of the Earl of Caithness, though there were problems about finding their dowries on time, and then the sons-in-law were not wholly satisfactory, leaving the old man to bring up and educate his grandchildren. Nor were his own three sons at all satisfactory. John the Master of Tarbat who became the second Earl on his father's death in 1714 had been a very dashing sprig, a Restoration Buck of the first water in Edinburgh. His first marriage to Lady Eliza Gordon had ended in divorce: he blamed his wife's extravagance; she claimed that she had been *left in pawn*, as surety for debts they had jointly incurred in the Low Country, while John returned to Scotland, and she had perforce accepted the protection of another man. John soon married again—Mary Murray, a girl who has not left much trace in the Papers: she was the mother of John's son and heir George, later the third earl, and his brother Roderick. John had been involved in a thundering scandal in Edinburgh, a drunken frolic complete with scampering serving-wenches, ended in an affray in which a Frenchman was run through with a sword in the darkened bedroom of a tavern in Leith occupied by John and friends. It took all the political influence and forensic agility with which his father was so well endowed to get the Master off a charge of murder, compounded, as it was, with a whiff of treason. Why did John frequent a harbour inn used by a Frenchman, at a time when any contact with France was suspect because of the exile there of the former King James, that personal friend and patron of the house of Tarbat? The Master was exiled to the Low Country for a while, and then remained in permanent residence in Ross, though whether this was a tacit condition of the government, or exile imposed by his old father is not at all clear. It was not until after

3 Lady Elizabeth Gordon, first wife of the Master of Tarbat, a Restoration waif divorced for extravagances for which she was not wholly to blame.

5 Maria Murray, second wife of The Master and mother of George the heir. The pair of portraits were painted about 1704, shortly after their marriage.

4 John Master of Tarbat as a young man in the pink of fashion. His major creditor was his tailor. He became the second Earl in 1714.

the death of the first Earl nearly 20 years later that his son went south again.

The Master did not settle entirely to the quiet life of a country gentleman, as he took an active and embarrassing part in the new party just beginning to be called 'Jacobite', after the exiled King James. As his father was at the same time attempting to establish his own credibility at the court of King William at Kensington, and was indeed appointed as the new King's expert adviser on Highland affairs, the actions of his son in support of Dundee and in planned military forays with his kinsman Lord Lovat were inopportune. General Mackay put The Master under arrest in Inverness for a short spell. Still worse, The Master became an adherent of the Church of Rome, and offered a clandestine 'safe house' for the few priests still venturing into the north to minister to their scattered flocks, all of whom were deeply suspected of Jacobite sympathies, and perhaps with good reason. The first Earl wrote a long closely-argued letter at this time, presumably to his son, although there is no date nor superscription, trying to dissuade him from leaving the episcopalian protestant church of his upbringing for Rome. None of the rest of the Mackenzies of Cromartie seem to have followed the Master of Tarbat to Rome, though the family of his cousins the Mackenzies of Seaforth were adherents.

The newly expanded territories of Lord Tarbat, after he had received the Charter of Cromarty, and the Sheriffdom had been confirmed in 1686, did not remain formally in his possession for very long. Almost immediately he made elaborate settlements: Tarbat House and Barony went to his eldest son, The Master: Cromarty to his second son, Kenneth, reserving to himself only the Sheriffdom and the use of the new warehouse—the Girnel of Cromarty—which he had just had built (as at Portmahomack), where the arm of the harbour joined the shore. Royston House went, nominally, to his son James, reserving a life-interest for himself. His sons were all young at the time of the settlement: James was still under age, a slightly wayward scholar at Oxford. It is not clear why Lord Tarbat settled his properties on his sons in this unusual way during his own vigorous lifetime. He lived another twenty years. Possibly it may have been an endeavour to preserve the estates for the family, as financial embarrassments were growing and came to a crisis in 1704 when a number of creditors put pressure on The Master, and indirectly on his father. The whole family had acquired a very expensive style of living, as some of their remaining bills show. The first Earl himself had excellent and educated, but alas expensive, taste. He had, after the long illness of his first wife who died in 1699, remarried. His bride was the dowager countess of Wemyss. He courted her in the style of a young cavalier, gave her lavish presents, had her portrait painted and engraved, and took her to London when he was the greatest officer of state in Scotland, the Queen's Secretary for

Scotland. When she died there suddenly he mourned her, and organised a lavish funeral in Scotland and a memorial in St Margaret's church, Westminster. It is not certain how long after her death that he took a gentlewoman into his keeping, but Mistress Frances Walker remained with him until his death in 1714, acknowledged by his family.

The first Earl had a host of friends, and Fraser published letters about hunting parties, the exchange of hounds, deer-hunting, horses, the affairs of the Royal Company of Archers and much else. There are many letters exchanged with politically-minded peers, and others from Ministers and clergy of the episcopalian persuasion. The Earl was patron for fourteen parishes in Ross, the former benefices of the Bishops whose Teinds (tithes) his family had added to their income through a royal grant. This involved him closely in Kirk affairs at a time when the north of Scotland was still divided between those of presbyterian inclination and those, like the earl himself, who preferred a liturgy and to keep the ancient festivals of the Church's year. The dividing line was a fine one.

Students of Scottish theology in the seventeenth century, as well as those interested in politics, might well take another look at Tarbat, first Earl of Cromartie, and the affairs of Ross. At the time of William and Mary's accession in 1688 there was a strong pro-Jacobite party, as we have seen in connection with the Master. A Williamite, or Government military command under General MacKay of Scourie, was set up with headquarters in Inverness, quartering troops at points of suspected disaffection all over the Highlands; Lord Tarbat was in London advising William on Highland affairs. Queen Mary was an old friend. There was thought to be none to match Tarbat's intimate knowledge of affairs in the north in spite of being known as a former adherent of King James, and his proposals had a faint chance of reconciling the disaffected clans to the new monarchs. Unfortunately Tarbat and these families accurately saw the greatest threat to their own lands and powers as coming from the family of Campbell of Argyll, a family then bent on aggrandisement. Tarbat was out-manoeuvred and dismissed from Royal favour and the Earl of Argyll himself had the royal ear. 'The old fox', Breadalbane, got Tarbat's position. (William was said to be indifferent to Scottish affairs and only wanted the country kept quiet and able to contribute taxes and men to his annual campaigns in the Low Country against the King of France.) One of the consequences of this shift of royal favour was the massacre of Glen Coe. The government's locally recruited militia and troops quartered in Ross did not perpetrate any such dire injustice, but to provide their food and forage was a heavy burden on the estates of the earl and his neighbours, numbers of whom wrote to him asking him to protect 'this poor country' of Ross. Local power was then in the hands of the Sheriff of Ross, the Laird of Balnagowan, a man much disliked by the Mackenzie families, though General Mackay retained their goodwill. Mackay listened patiently to the complaints of the Heritors of Ross that the orders to provide armed and mounted men to augment the army were burdensome and unnecessary as 'no Highlandmen had been seen in these parishes'. Even as far north as Tain and Dingwall men did not believe that they themselves were 'Highlandmen' even though the folk were all Gaelic speakers. Highlandmen were 'clannit men' and hailed from the west, and in the days before any connecting roads were made, it was only the annual cattlefairs at Beauly and Muir of Ord, or the feared raising of war-bands (in a manner already considered old-fashioned and lawless), which brought 'clannit men' over.

One of the most notable general characteristics which emerged from the perusal of Lord Tarbat's correspondence with his neighbours and the great network of Mackenzie kin, who owned many of the best properties in the Black Isle and Easter Ross, is the new emphasis on legal means for obtaining just ends. On the whole, the community longed to be law-abiding, but it was sometimes hard to distinguish where power lay. For example, a tenant of Tarbat's wrote to him in Edinburgh in high indignation that the men of Glen Urquhart had raided and removed his cattle from Strathpeffer; could he raise a force of local men to repossess them? Tarbat instead made him raise an action in Inverness Sheriff Court— which incidentally took three years to settle. The case was, all the same, an indication that the rough justice of raiding and counter-raiding was nearly over: the future lay with the observation of the law.

Well placed and senior members of the clan living in the capital, such as Tarbat and Rosehaugh who held the highest judicial offices, were obviously an asset to the whole Mackenzie connection, but almost equally important were solicitors such as Mackenzie of Delvine, in Edinburgh. The control of Ministers and schoolmasters in fourteen parishes out of the twenty-two of Ross reinforced social control. It was the use of local legal power which made the rule of Sheriff Ross of Balnagowan so irksome; the magnates of the house of Mackenzie could have taken orders with more grace from one of their own kin. They suspected Balnagowan of private gain and vendetta. When General Mackay was taxed with making such an inappropriate appointment he replied blandly that 'none of the name of Mackenzie' had offered himself for office and Balnagowan had. Both Ross of Balnagowan and the head of the other great rival family in Easter Ross, Munro of Foulis, had early declared for strict presbyterian church order and for King William, and later for the House of Hanover. The Mackenzies were much greater supporters of the old House of Stuart, and held firmly to protestant episcopalian church management. Over two generations Clan Mackenzie suffered from the behaviour of the head of the clan: Seaforth became Roman Catholic, as well as remaining a Jacobite.

When the young heir was sent to France to get a catholic education in 1694, fourteen of his Mackenzie kinsmen wrote to Lord Tarbat (next to Seaforth in seniority), to implore him to get the boy back to be educated in Scotland as a protestant. By the time of the Jacobite Risings of 1715, 1719, and the much later 1745–46 Rising, the cohesiveness of Clan Mackenzie was gone, split on religious and political affiliations, and Balnagowan, Munro of Foulis, and other families in Ross had begun to dominate local as well as national affairs. They had backed the winners.

In spite of his chronic financial problems, and the national trauma, the first Earl continued to be a leading figure in Ross and in Scottish affairs in general until his retirement from public affairs in 1712, in his eightieth year. He spent most of the last years of his life in Castle Leod, surrounded by his library, his charter chests, his vast correspondence, and the many lists of his own making. He was disappointed in his heir, but devoted to his eldest grandson and namesake George, son of John and Mary Murray. He left a Will in his grandson's favour which only gave a life-rent of the Barony and mansion house of Tarbat to his son John, who thus had no legal right whatever to 'sell, dispone or otherwise dispose' of any of the lands or produce. George was a minor at his grandfather's death, and his father was put into the invidious position of being Tutor or guardian to his own son, but without the power to sell his son's property for his own gain. This predictably did not prevent John from *trying* to raise money for himself by the sale of his son's possessions, as was the case in the matter of the standing timber of Coigach.

John was always desperately straitened for money. It is not clear how he spent it: some bills for drink and books and from tailors survive, but many accounts from this period are lost. Even in his father's lifetime the family had to part with the best cornlands in the parish of Tarbat to their tenant and distant kinsman, Macleod of Cadboll, to pay off John's debts. The lands of Easter Aird were wadset and Macleod had lent his landlord a great deal of money. In 1704 he claimed some lands in repayment, and took on the lease and management of the Barony of Strathpeffer, on tack. Again in 1727, during another major crisis, and once more after the third earl's whole estate was forfeited to the Crown in the Rising of 1745, Macleod claimed more land, and laid a firm foundation for his own family on the ruins of the Earl's holdings in Tarbat. In the crisis of 1727 a number of creditors of the second Earl and even some bearing bonds of the first Earl, still unredeemed, joined in legal processes to have the second Earl declared a bankrupt. A petition handed in by one George Jamieson, Candlemaker in Canongate to the Lords of Session was

> for himself and as Trustee for a GREAT number of poor people in and about Edinburgh such as merchants, writers, landlords, periwig makers, Tailors,

Shoemakers, fleshers, baxters, Poultrymen, Brewers, slater, stabling, saddlers, Wrights, Episcopal ministers, chaplain, cook and others having furnished to the RT. Hon John Earl of Cromartie and his family while residing in Edinburgh and to some of his children while at school and colleges, goods merchandise and lodging money and other necessaries even things of the Lowest Denomination not fit to be mentioned ...

It was a desperate list.

Only the marriage of his son George, afterwards the third Earl, saved the estate. During this crisis, the Earl, with his third wife, left for London where perhaps, for a time, credit was easier to obtain for an unknown Scottish earl. Characteristically he invested heavily at this time in the South Sea Bubble and kept the share to prove it. The new Countess of Cromartie was a Fraser, married and widowed twice before, and evidently it had been hoped by the other relations that she could control the unstable and now elderly earl. Perhaps she did; there are sadly few letters preserved from this stage of the family saga. The third marriage was more prolific than the second; there were six half-brothers and four half-sisters in the brood at Tarbat House by the time the second earl died, aged about 65, in 1731. George, now the third Earl, made the minimum legal provision for the dowager countess and her children; he remained on good terms with his half-brothers. His own marriage in 1726 was to Bonnie Bel Gordon, Mistress Isabella Gordon, daughter of Sir William Gordon of Invergordon.

It may have been a marriage prudently arranged by his uncle Lord Elibank with the daughter of a prosperous neighbour and a leading Whig supporter of King George II; all the same it was a love match, and lasted through great vicissitudes. Bonny Bel's last child was born in the Tower of London with her husband under sentence of death for his part in the Jacobite Rising of 1745. Twenty years before that the third earl and his countess had come into possession of Castle Leod and Tarbat House, both then pretty derelict with farm lands run down and rack-rented. The Earl put in hand a few good measures of land improvement, and began to reorganise his tenants' holdings. Bonny Bel set the two houses to rights, had them papered and painted and new furnished, and her father paid off the worst of the family debts, dating to Earl John's day, but unfortunately not all were paid. There are delightful pictures of the young children of Earl George and Lady Isabella hanging among the more stern family portraits.

But however prosperous the picture seemed there were storms ahead. One had been brewing for a long time. As a result of the impoverished condition of the second Earl, the third had somehow neglected to clear the dues outstanding to the Crown in respect of his Estate. The annual

Crown Rents were due for the past twenty years or so, and in spring 1745 the Treasury tax-gatherers began to send most ominous letters, eventually threatening dispossession from the whole estate if the back dues were not met. The sum required was over £7,000 sterling, more than the total rental for five years from the whole estate. It presented an almost insuperable problem to raise such a sum. Simultaneously another long-heralded storm broke, as news spread of the landing of The Young Chevalier, Prince Charles Edward, son of James The Old Chevalier. He arrived in August 1745 on the west coast of Inverness-shire, without the promised French support in arms and gold, and without, if truth be told, his father's endorsement of his venture. A series of dubious Jacobite agents had assured the Prince that the whole of Scotland only awaited his arrival to rise, and that England too awaited him. This was a gross overestimate. The Prince, on landing, wrote to the Highland lords of known Jacobite interest, including the Mackenzie connection, the young Seaforth—then known as Lord Fortrose as his father had forfeited the title in earlier Jacobite forays—and to the third Earl of Cromartie, grandson of that loyal supporter of the Stuart crown. (His father, the second Earl, had been dissuaded by practical men from joining Seaforth in the Rising of 1715 which ended at Sherrifmuir; he was deemed to be too unstable.) Earl George was in a hideous dilemma. His estates were only just beginning to recover from years of neglect; he was trying out some Improved agriculture; his father-in-law had long served as the private secretary and trusted advisor of Frederick, Prince of Wales, son of George II, who later predeceased his father. Though the king and the prince were on famously bad terms, they were both Hanoverian, and represented the established government. But the demand for the Crown Rents cast a doubt on the Earl's ability to continue in the enjoyment of his whole property. He played for time. No reply to the letter sent by Prince Charles Edward to his Trusted Cousin of Cromartie survives, and it is probable that no written reply was sent.

Immediately on the news of the Prince's landing becoming known in the north, the representative of the government of King George went into action. Lord President Duncan Forbes of Culloden was a loyal and able servant of the house of Hanover, and had the best interests of Scotland, as he saw them, at heart. He summoned the waverers to a house-party at Culloden House, near Inverness. At his right hand was Norman MacLeod of MacLeod, chief. He entertained Lord Fortrose, Lord Cromartie, Lord Lovat, Grant of Rothiemurchus and several others whose loyalty was important, and undisclosed.

All these magnates were united not only by close blood-ties but also by ties of common interest. After a couple of months of wavering, Fortrose and Grant remained firm to the Hanoverian government while Lovat and his nephew Cromartie started raising men to form two regiments, without at first saying whose cause they had espoused. They showed their hands when they recruited over their own boundaries into the lands of Grant whose Glen Urquhart and Morrison clansmen were known Jacobites, episcopalian and disgusted with their Laird's adherence to Hanover. Cromartie raised a whole Regiment, and marched with Lovat and his force to join the army of the Prince in Perth in November 1745. Cromartie's eldest son John Lord MacLeod went with him. Like his great-grandfather at the Battle of Worcester, he was just eighteen.

Cromartie was sent to reinforce the Chief of Clan Cameron, Locheil, who was in command of the Fords of Forth; they had a raggle-taggle band of Clan McGregor garrisoning the Fords from bases in Doune and Dunblane. Cromartie and Lochiel spent the winter patrolling what had become the frontier between the risen Highlands, and the Hanoverian rest of Britain. They stayed in the centrally placed house of Mistress McGregor of Balhaldie, Lochiel's sister, in Dunblane, and Cromartie attempted to raise money and horses for the Prince from the neighbouring lairds. The Prince and the main army had swept through, to the occupation of Edinburgh, the successful battle of Prestonpans, and the desperate venture of the march south. Late in December the Prince's army turned back at Derby, disheartened by lack of English support. The Government had sent to Germany for King George's able military son, William Duke of Cumberland, to take command of the reinforced Hanoverian army. The retreating Jacobites met the vanguard of this army and inflicted a sharp defeat on it at Falkirk, an action in which the Earl and his eldest son both fought with distinction. But there was only one way out, north to their bases. Cumberland had landed at Leith and was just eight days march behind the Jacobite army. This split into three sections. Cromartie's regiment was sent north through Drumochter and on into Ross where he was appointed commander 'be north the Beauly river' by the Prince. Cromartie's brief was to raise men, horses and supplies in Ross, and to meet, if possible, a French frigate said to be bound for the north with cannon and gold. They had a measure of success, causing such alarm in Inverness that Lord President Forbes of Culloden and his ally Norman MacLeod of MacLeod left in disguise to go into hiding on Skye. No French frigate was seen, only the pervasive English patrols of HM's Navy. Cromartie's command, like the rest of the Jacobite army's, was bedevilled by contrary instructions coming from the Prince's Irish advisors, and, in a confused skirmish at the gates of Dunrobin in Sutherland, Cromartie, his son John and a number of his Regiment were taken prisoner—some were killed. It was the evening before the final battle of the Rising was fought on the Lord President's estate of Culloden, on 15 April 1746.

The documents which illustrate this terribly troubled period have nearly all long been published in various reports of the Forty-Five. As this is a family scrap book, the few details repeated here concentrate on how participation in the Rising affected the family of the Earl.

After the surrender at Dunrobin he and his son were parted, the Earl to go straight to London in a ship of the navy. Under the charge of High Treason he and the three other Scottish Lords taken prisoner were confined in the Tower of London. John Lord MacLeod, also arraigned for High Treason, was put into one of the hulks moored in the Thames, along with other officer prisoners. The men were mostly taken to Carlisle where they were tried before the nearest English jury—thought more likely to convict than a Scottish jury—and transported to the West Indies. Some were hung. Cromartie's Regiment was mostly composed of 'clannit men' from Coigach in the west. Few could even speak English or understand their trial. Very few returned home.

It seems that Bonnie Bel remained at New Tarbat House during the winter campaign: her husband actually made it his base in March 1746 when he was in command in the north. When he was imprisoned in April she went first to Edinburgh with her three eldest daughters, whom she left in the house of the family lawyer, Leonard Urquhart, WS. She then rode in great haste with only a young ghillie to accompany her, all the way to London where she joined her husband in his imprisonment. The ghillie, whose name is now forgotten, lived to a great age and was fond of recounting his part in the dramatic rush to London. The four younger children were left in Tarbat House under the care of Mistress Mackenzie of Meddat, wife to the third generation of Meddat chamberlains to the house of Cromartie. Their fates are recounted in the chapter on the children.

John Mackenzie of Meddat held the estate together through the years of its forfeiture to the Crown, dying in 1784 the year the estate was restored to John Lord MacLeod, nearly forty years after he had first set out with his father as a boy of 18. There are a great number of surviving letters exchanged between the earl and Meddat, up to the time of the earl's death in London in 1766. On the very eve of execution the Earl was pardoned by the Crown at the instigation of Frederick Prince of Wales (whose trusted secretary was Sir William Gordon, father of Bonnie Bel). The portrait of 'Poor Fred', the Prince of Wales, is the only Hanoverian face among all the portraits still in the family possession. Dramatic stories were current at the time and since of the Countess of Cromartie, heavily pregnant and 'surrounded by her ten young children' falling at the King's feet to present her petition, thus obtaining the royal pardon. She certainly gave birth to her last child in the Tower, but she did not have all her own brood around her. Perhaps she borrowed some nieces and nephews in the interests of a picturesque scene.

Some of the most interesting letters show that the lawyer Urquhart had

6 'Poor Fred', Frederick Prince of Wales, son of George II and father of George III, who took up the Cromartie cause to annoy his father and at the urging of his secretary, Sir William Gordon, father of Bonnie Bel.

the older girls in Edinburgh until the Earl's release in 1748. The littlest girls stayed at Tarbat for some years. The earl and countess were exiled for life in England, first at Honiton—from where he wrote pathetically that he would exchange all the cider in Devon for a stoup of whisky, and asked Meddat to send a barrel of salt herring from Ullapool, and some oatmeal and honey. After a short spell there he and his family returned to London for the rest of their long and straitened exile. Meantime the estates were annexed 'in perpetuity' to the Crown, the furniture was sold from the houses, troops were billeted in Castle Leod, and Tarbat House with its beautiful gardens fell into ruin and was vandalised. Lord John MacLeod and his brother George ran away from the Devon home and joined the mercenary army of the protestant King of Sweden. George came back to England after his father had persuaded his kinsman General Murray to take him into the royal army in Canada. George went to Quebec, and served all his life as a soldier of King George, but John remained for twenty-five years hard campaigning in the service of the King of Sweden and the King of Prussia, in their armies. He showed great military ability, and rose to be made a Count of Sweden, and a Marshal of the Swedish Army. Many other Scots had followed the example of Marshal Keith and served in the protestant armies of Northern Europe, locked perennially in warfare against the Catholic Emperor and the Bourbon King. Lord MacLeod was deeply involved in the construction of the gigantic for-tification of Sveaborg, built by Sweden to guard her Eastern approaches, in the formal and heavily-fortified style of Vauban. Advances in the transport of heavy artillery were already rendering such massive forts obsolete. Curiously, the nearest British equivalent to Sveaborg is Fort George, built near Inverness at about the same time, a magnificent monu-ment to Hanoverian fears of further Jacobite Risings in the North. But there were no more Risings.

Lovat's heir pointed the way for the Forfeited and Attainted magnates to re-establish themselves in Government favour, and ultimately to get their estates back. He raised a regiment of Frasers to fight in the colonial wars in which Britain and France were locked for most of the eighteenth century, and thus regained favour, and the Lovat Estates. In 1761, before the death of George, the 'former' Earl (for nearly twenty years simply described as *The Attaindered Person* in official references) his son John Mackenzie, (called Lord MacLeod out of courtesy only) attempted to get permission to raise a regiment as Lovat had done. Urquhart, the family solicitor, tried his best; the opinion of that smart young Advocate Mr James Boswell was also sought, but the Crown remained adamant until 1774, when letters from the Queen-Regent of Sweden, and those of Henry Dundas, another legal family friend and relative, had some force. Henry Dundas was beginning his career of influence in Scottish affairs, which eventually took him to the top of the tree as Secretary of State for Scotland, and the nickname of 'King Henry IX'.

Mr John Mackenzie (*sic*) and his brother Major George Mackenzie were sanctioned to raise a regiment of Highland foot. It is not clear whether Lord MacLeod had ever been north since he had been taken prisoner at Dunrobin in 1746. He stood as Member of Parliament for Ross Burghs in his absence, as part of a more than usually convoluted piece of political intrigue which involved Elibank, Henry Dundas, Pulteney (later of Bath) and, in opposition of course, Munro of Foulis. As all the Cromartie estates were still 'inalienably' annexed to the Crown, it is difficult to see how MacLeod was qualified as a candidate, but apparently his Uncle Gordon made over some land near Invergordon to him. During the long period between 1746 and the eventual return in 1784 the estates were administered by The Commissioners For the Forfeited and Annexed Estates, and an account of their stewardship is given in Richards and Clough's *Cromartie: Highland Life*. Only a few of the many letters written by the Factor at that time are quoted here, where they refer to the houses or furnishings of the family.

In 1774 the two Mackenzie brothers were apparently welcomed with open arms by the tenantry, and had no difficulty in recruiting what was first called *Lord MacLeod's Regiment of Foot*, raised mainly from the tenants of Coigach whose fathers had suffered so heavily in Lord Cromartie's Regiment, in the Prince's cause. The regiment was embodied at a ceremony in Elgin under the Army listing of The 74th Foot, afterwards renumbered as the 71st Foot, and eventually to become The Highland Light Infantry. Many of the neighbouring lairds were also raising regiments, so much so that there was a shortage of the tall men who went to make up line regiments. In MacLeod's case the height limit for recruits was 'not below' 5'6", light infantry indeed. The record of all the Highland regiments then raised was a brilliant one in war, and a deplorable one in peace. For one thing men who had never left Wester Ross were easy victims to the unfamiliar diseases of urban Britain; even measles left whole companies depleted. Far harder to bear were the broken promises of many of the officers raising and commanding these new clan-based regiments; promises to remain always at the head of their men were hardly ever kept, and jumped-up minor tacksmen or still worse, English officers and NCOs who could not speak Gaelic at all, were put in command. It is much to the credit of Lord MacLeod and his brother that they remained at the head of their regiment which was thus one of the few—perhaps the only— Highland regiment of the period which never suffered a mutiny of its men. These mutinies were nearly always occasioned by a posting to the West Indies where fever killed more than any warfare, and first-class officers were reluctant to go. MacLeod commanded the 1st Battalion when it left England for South India in 1782. MacLeod and his men took a salient part in the capture of Goree from the French, on the west coast of Africa, as their first engagement on the way to India. His brother George raised a 2nd Battalion which followed, after taking part in a stirring action at Gibraltar.

Once landed in Madras they took part in the war against Hyder Ali, under the command of General Eyre Coote, an irascible old veteran with whom MacLeod eventually quarrelled on the grounds that his troops were treated inferiorly, and were inadequately housed and fed. Lord MacLeod now got his full courtesy title in civilly expressed letters from the Secretary of State for War. He returned to Britain after a couple of years where Urquhart was finally negotiating the return of the Cromartie Estates. His brother George remained as full colonel in command of the Regiment; however he died of a tropical fever soon after, and is buried under a handsome obelisk in the Fort Cemetry, Madras.

Lord MacLeod was able to take possession of the Cromartie estates on his landing. The Crown demanded payment of the £7,000 Crown rents due since 1731 or so: tax gatherers never give up. The Crown had ironically kept the estates intact and even marginally improved during the long annexation. MacLeod was a grizzled veteran of forty years campaigning from the arctic snows of Lapland to the plains of Madras. He sat for his portrait to Romney, and also had him paint the bride he took on his return, Marjorie Forbes. They found New Tarbat House so ruinous that it was decided to demolish it, and to rebuild in the purest classical mode of the day. Some of the old furniture, the family papers and the portraits were restored by the agent of his uncle William Gordon of Invergordon, whose heir MacLeod had become. But the old life and the old relationships had begun to change out of recognition.

All the work of his ancestors had been allowed to decay, the mansion house was partly roofless, the gardens were overgrown with scrub and vandalised by the local lads who had helped themselves to bits of the first Earl's cherished lead statues—lead after all can be melted into useful musket-balls. This book and the Papers on which it is based are now the only record of the old mansion of New Tarbat, which was once so fine.

The house which took its place, and which actually may incorporate some of the masonry of the 1680s building, was an extremely elegant and regular classically designed house with large light rooms and finely moulded ceilings, a staircase that sprang lightly from the square central hall to a fine first floor, and to a second floor supported on ascending pillars of the three Greek orders. The plaster work departed from the strictly classical only in one tiny detail, the orthodox ox-skull pattern between swags of anthemion, was subtly replaced by antlered deer skulls, an allusion to the Mackenzie badge. The walls were plastered and panelled to frame the portraits of ancestors from Sir Rory the Tutor painted by Jamieson to the new pictures by Romney of Lord MacLeod and his wife. The faithful steward of Invergordon produced the pictures, and much of the old furniture which had been hidden away, together with the Charters and Papers. The architect of Tarbat was James McLeran, and his careful plans of 1796 still exist for the guidance of a new generation of architects.

Tarbat House (confusingly no longer called New Tarbat although it had superseded the former New Tarbat) continued to be the chief residence of the family until 1962. Since then it has several times changed hands, belonging for a time to the rival Balnagowan Estates, which would have horrified its first builder and certainly did nothing for the fabric of the building, which was allowed to deteriorate and to offer a haven for a new generation of vandals until quite recently when, after a fire which almost totally destroyed it, new owners have taken the lovely building in hand and restoration is in progress. The great walled garden has only a few stark roses and lichenous apple trees among the undergrowth to mark one of the best gardens in the north.

Lord MacLeod never enjoyed his new house, dying before it was finished. His nephew and heir by entail, Captain Kenneth Mackenzie (son of Roderick, the third Earl's next brother), only lived for a short period after inheriting, and died without legitimate children; he made provision for a son and daughter born out of wedlock in London. Isabella, the eldest daughter of the third earl, who had looked after her parents and the younger children in the long years of exile, returned to the new house of Tarbat bringing continuity with the old line. She was now Lady Elibank. It is thought that she did not live continuously at Tarbat, but preferred her husband's home in the Lowlands. However we know that she did spend some time at Tarbat, and tried to gather up the old links; even the question of exerting Kirk patronage, and of reviving the old Fishings of Conan occupied her and her daughter who succeeded her.

The family titles were still Forfeit, and though each succeeding generation made legal inquiry they remained in abeyance until Isabella, Lady Elibank's great-grand daughter and heir-direct, became the Duchess of Sutherland. She was Anne Hay-Mackenzie who had inherited the Cromartie Estates in her own right. Queen Victoria bestowed the titles again on her favourite Mistress of Robes, and by royal decree she became Countess of Cromartie in her own line. The Cromartie titles were entailed on her second son who thus re-established the earls of Cromartie, independent of the Sutherland line.

Of the town of Cromarty itself there is little information since the papers are missing. Soon after possession of the Urquhart Estates and the Burgh of Cromarty were confirmed by Royal Charter of James VII and II under the Great Seal in 1686, George Mackenzie, newly created Viscount

Tarbat, made over these properties to his second son, now Sir Kenneth Mackenzie. The castle of Cromarty was ruinous after years of Urquhart neglect, but Sir Kenneth and his lady lived there for part of each year, and he oversaw some of the grain shipments of his father. This was based on sailings of freighters from Cromarty to Leith until after 1720 when much of the surplus bere barley of Easter Ross was more profitably sold to the distillery of Ferintosh near Dingwall, the property of Forbes of Culloden. Sir Kenneth (the Factors complained he 'meddled' with estate business) was elected member for Cromarty of the Scots Parliament, and sat through the Union Parliament of 1707, later taking his seat in Westminster. He sat until his death in 1721, when he was succeeded in his honours, lands and parliamentary seat by his son Sir George. Neither father nor son have left much trace in the family records, and very little mark on the town, although both represented Cromarty in parliament. Painted panels of their Heraldic emblazons were in the parish church of Cromarty until recently, reused in a negligent way as part of the panels of the gallery. In recent restoration work they were removed, and their present whereabouts is unknown. The panels may have been part of an order from Lord Tarbat to the Heralds' College in Edinburgh for coats of arms, when he was raised to the rank of earl in 1704.

Sir George Mackenzie had a reputation for heavy drinking. He married a daughter of Skipper Reid, one of the most reliable of the Leith skippers in the corn trade, and a man who eventually settled in Cromarty. Eventually the run-down estate was bought by a Captain Urquhart, a colourful seafaring connection of the original owners.

The history of Royston House in Cromartie ownership is also a short one, for it was sold by the son of James Lord Royston to the Duke of Argyll in 1739. The Duke, riding high in Hanoverian favour, renamed it Caroline Park after the Queen and his own eldest daughter. Although work was done on the interior and on the stable block they do not seem to have lived there very much. It still stands foursquare near the beach of Granton, much as it was in Cromartie's day.

Some other loose ends should be tucked in: there is little mention in this book of the two other baronies which with Tarbat made up the estates of Cromartie and indeed the County of Cromarty. The Barony of Coigach in the northwest of Ross was always very different from the other properties. It was truly 'Highland' and the people were clannish Mackenzies and MacLeods following an archaic pattern of life. They were cattle raising pastoral people who came east once a year, at Martinmas, to the civilisation of Beauly market to sell their beasts and to pay their rents in good coin— 'silver mail' (the right side of the coin to 'blackmail' in its original sense of protection-money levied against cattle-rustling). The Barony of Coigach, which did not even have a baronial mansion or castle on it, and where

Baronial courts of justice were seldom held, deserves fuller and different treatment than can be given here.

The Barony of Strathpeffer is yet another story and one with a happier present day chapter for the family of Mackenzie of Tarbat. The Earl's flag as Cabarfeidh, Chief of Clan Mackenzie still flies over the tower built in the late sixteenth century. The doorway added by the Tutor when he married the heiress Margaret MacLeod from Coigach still stands hospitably open to clansmen and friends from all over the world. Castle Leod has always been the favourite, but not until recently the principal home of the family. It stands in mainly marginal land, between the corn of Tarbat and the pastures of Coigach. It was the sanctuary to which the old earl George retreated to die in 1714, a house in which his son and grandson often stayed, making no significant alterations. During the occupation by the Forfeited Estates Commissioners Castle Leod was used to billet the troops who were policing the country, and thus escaped destruction. Meddat the Chamberlain used the floor of the Great Room to take in the rents and girnel the bere barley in the difficult days directly after the Rising. Peter May, government surveyor, made an admirable map of the Barony in 1754, and the castle was returned intact in 1784, on Lord MacLeod's return to the estates. Only a little patch of pink ochre lime-wash survives on an inner face of the tower to show that the castle was pink-washed all over to indicate that it belonged to proven Jacobites, as was the practice during the policing after the Rising.

The Hanging Tree on which malefactors were despatched by the Barony Court has long died and the stump (it was Ash, of course) is covered by a rose-briar.

Reading the letters and Inventars, the rentals, bills and charters, the cookery receipts, the sermons and the military docquets in that house has been a privilege.

The Children of Three Generations

The children of the first Earl did not spend their early years either at Tarbat or at Royston: the former was in course of building and Royston was not acquired until the family were grown up. Not much is known about their early days in any event. Roderick, the eldest was an early casualty, and his place as Heir was taken by the next boy, John, Master of Tarbat, and later called Lord MacLeod as his father's career prospered. He was born about 1655 and followed by Kenneth and James and four sisters. Their time was divided between Castle Leod, Castle Ballone in Tarbat, and the lodgings in Edinburgh which their father kept in Old School Wynd. During the period of the Duke of York's residence in Scotland at the end of the 1670s Lord Tarbat as Lord Register had lodgings in Holyrood Palace itself. The children may have come in for some reflected glory, but it is unlikely that they stayed in the Royal palace themselves. Kenneth and James eventually went to Oxford, where some of the Scottish professors in the university kept an eye on them. Professor Gregorie and Professor Saville both wrote about them. Neither of the younger boys was a good scholar: James got into trouble with a woman (who blamed her maidservant) and was sent off to the Low Country to cool off. James afterwards had a good legal career in Edinburgh. The Master of Tarbat and his first wife also spent an expensive period abroad after the affray in the inn in Leith had made the Master's presence in Edinburgh inadvisable. Even less is known about the daughters of this generation, except for their marriages—on paper both suitable and prosperous. Unfortunately the eldest, who married Bruce of Clackmannan, saw her husband bankrupt before long. The family of Brown of Coalston, into whom the second daughter married, were among those who later sued the second earl, her brother, for money he long owed them. Her father paid for the education of his two Brown grandchildren. Lady Clackmannan had to return to her father's roof. Lady Jean, the third daughter married Stewart of Balcaskie, a fairly disastrous marriage. For a long period, when she was an elderly widow, she was confined with severe mental trouble in the house of the Minister of Loch Broom, distant enough from censorious gossip. The letters of the Minister reveal him and his wife showing great charity towards a difficult charge. Perhaps she was the daughter who had the reputation of swashbuckling about Edinburgh wearing a mannish cloak, and using most independent language, though the reference is more likely to be to the youngest daughter, for long her father's companion, the Lady Anne who eventually married a cousin, Major John Sinclair. Allowances were secured on all the daughters, and were paid fairly regularly, forming quite a heavy charge on the estate. Only a few of their receipts survive. One for example was from Lady Jean Stewart of Balcaskie for £35 sterling 'in part payment of my annuity' in 1700. It seems from remaining indications that it was a handsome amount, for the day. Four receipts for 1704 and 1705 indicate that Lady Anna Sinclair received £200 Scots each half year from her father, and in 1708 Lady Jean Stewart gave receipt for 1,400 merks from Cadboll—the tacksman of Castle Leod at that point— and a further 800 merks from her father, for the years 1704 and 1705: on the reverse side the lady had somewhat tartly written 'Reserving the action against my brother Sir Kenneth for what he may be found lyable to me for preceeding years'. No family love lost it appears, and four years in arrears. Restoration Britain was a chancy place to be young in, and a father who was clawing his way up the slippery ladder of royal favour had apparently little time to spare on child-guidance.

The first children to emerge with identities of their own, and with strong associations with Tarbat and Royston are the children of Earl John, and his second wife Maria Murray, Lord Elibank's daughter. They were George, the eldest and heir, born in 1702, and Roderick, always a close pair in boyhood. They were followed by another pair, William and Peter (or Patrick—he was called both). That there were others who did not survive is painfully clear.

In June 1714 the old Earl was at Castle Leod and his son was away on family business in the western barony of Coigach, waiting for the arrival of two ships with stores for the fishing station that he and his father had been trying to establish on the shores of Loch Broom. John Tarbat wrote to his father saying he had been called home to New Tarbat by two express letters from his wife containing the sad news that she herself was indisposed

> and has had her blood let in an extremity, and that Nellie and Gideon having after recovery from the small pox, contracted the chin cough (whooping cough) whereof, and of teething, the later dyed. Nellie is weak and hectick, her cough violent, and Will and Peter are unaisie by it: only George and Roric are as yet free.

There is no other mention of Nellie in the family papers, so perhaps she did not survive the twin scourges of small-pox and whooping cough either. Peter and William did. Their mother Countess Mary died soon

after, in 1716, after a long illness, and Earl John then went south to
Edinburgh where eventually his relatives found him a suitable and strong-
minded third wife in Anna Fraser of Lovat, twice widowed herself after
marriages to Fotheringham of Powrie and to Norman MacLeod of
MacLeod. By the time she took on the elderly second earl and his four
sons the estates were very embarrassed. She and Earl John lived away from
the north, partly in Edinburgh at Royston and partly in London, leaving
the children in the care of a nurse, Grizzel, and the boys nominally under
the chamberlain's charge. Lord Elibank was appointed a guardian to his
late sister's eldest son, and he and another sister, Lady Mackenzie of Coul
made occasional attempts to keep an eye on the two eldest boys. The third
Countess produced several children after this; there is even less known
about them than there is of the older family, but we know from his letters
that Sir Norman MacLeod, their mother's son by her second marriage,
'had a kindness' for his little half-brothers and sisters, and helped them in
later life.

George and Roderick, the two eldest boys had a tutor, or 'governor'
appointed for a time, a young student of medicine from the University
of Aberdeen called James Mackenzie who afterwards had a distinguished
medical career, finally founding Worcester Infirmary, in England. He was
not in charge for long, however, and early in 1717 when George Lord
Tarbat would have been about fourteen, the chamberlain (confusingly
also called Norman McLeod) reported in a letter to their absent father that
Tarbat and Roderick had been sent to Inverness High School as boarders.
McLeod wrote that there had been a family party as a send-off, with Sir
Robert and Sir Kenneth Mackenzie (two uncles) and that they had gone
on to Coul, and from there he and the boys had gone to Inverness where
he left them:

> I heard from them last nyghtt and Blessed be God they are perffkly satisfyd
> with ebrything ... I ordered them to the ffrench school nyxt day after I got
> them fitted in thr. cloathes which I hope your lordship will not take amis
> since I ffolowed my lord Tarbat's inclination ... on the way his gobenor
> assured me that beffor the 5 March he would be capuble to discourse in the
> ffrench townghe. It will hinder none of their learning seeing I ordered Mr.
> La Marler to com to ther chamber only at such hour that the gobernor
> would direct.
>   The rest of your lordship's children with Grissel is berie well, I thank God,
> and had nebir a minutes uneasiness since your lordship left New Tarbatt. ...
> I must tell yor lordship that the nyght I stayed at Cowill (Coul) with the
> children that my lady Cowill spoke to me to order up her sister's clothes.

These were clothes that had belonged to the boys' mother the late Mary,
countess of Cromartie. Norman McLeod protested that he had had no

order from Earl John about the disposing of the late countess' clothes even
to her own sister and he had 'resolved not to allow anything to go without
the gaitte of New Tarbatt or Castle Leod without your lordship's personal
orders.' McLeod wrote a number of garulous letters, all betraying a dread
of offending the Earl. He nearly always mentions the children, and a clear
impression comes through of his care for the motherless boys, sent to
boarding school for the first time. McLeod's own son 'Normie' went with
them as body-servant or ghillie.

Exactly a year later Norman McLeod wrote to Earl John another long
letter about estate affairs, ending

> The children is all in verie good health blessed be to God, I had a letter from
> my Lord Tarbat this afternoon intreating the ffavour to remitt ffourteen
> shillings to him, ... to buy triffolls as he will, they are to have at Inverness
> this weeke, where he is to be King in the Barill, as Mr Cerigh (Carey?)
> wryte me. I could not refuse him which I hope your lordship will allow.

The 'King in the Barrel', a kind of elected Lord of Misrule, had a day's
rule of the school and had to hand out trifling presents.

Two months later the earl's brother James Mackenzie, now Lord
Royston, wrote to his uncle Roderick, Lord Prestonhall, the judge, about
a settlement of John Earl of Cromartie's affairs, to which he says Cromartie
had reluctantly concurred.

> He made a right to me of the Barony of Coygeach for the education of his
> two eldest sons, whith tho' little, not exceeding 2,000 merks, is yet better
> (than none) ... I was forced to engage my credit for a pretty round summ
> to bribe him to make this settlement.

The worthy chamberlain Norman McLeod collected the Coigach rents
and paid the rent of 1719 to Lord Royston, £50 sterling, in May. In June
McLeod began another long and scrambling letter to Earl John with an
apology: 'Knowing you dont like long letters ...', he details how much
the children are growing, and that they need new clothes.

> My wyfe broke [unpicked] two of her mother's silk gowens and a worstet
> one. my wyffe made two handsome gowns for each of them ... childrens is
> growing verie fast, perticularly Lady Mary. In the meantime I have sent the
> measure since your lordship called for it, and also the measure of the two
> yung gentlemen's heads for hatts, since not one can be had in this country.

Reverting to the younger children he goes on that

> Our schoolmaster has got a call to Cromarty and left, so (unless our children
> would forgitt what they learn) I have taken into the house a verie good lad

> a brother of James Mackenzie, that came from Aberdeen on Whitsunday
> and must go back at Martinmas, by which tyme I hope your lordship will
> be home and seen to the settlement yourself.

If the Earl and his new Countess did come home it was not for very
long, nor did they make any lasting arrangements for the education of the
four sons of his previous marriage. In 1721 another factotum, James Innes,
wrote in an even more illiterate hand than McLeod's, sending the Coigach
rents to the Earl (and not for education, it seems) adding

> all your children are well but long uerie much for the families homecoming.
> Mr William and Mr Patrick is at great loss for want of a governour for long
> ... Mr Rorie is gon south with my lady Coull and is thought My Lord
> Tarbatt is to go south uerie soon.

Cromartie was in the north from December 1721 to March 1722, during
which time his creditors finally succeeded in sequestering the rents of the
estate of Tarbat, having pursued him for years. It would not be characteristic of him to bother with engaging a tutor at such a crisis. In August
1722 Rorie, that is, Roderick Mackenzie, wrote to his father Earl John to
announce that he had come to Edinburgh to put his case in person. He
was about nineteen years old and sent a dignified and desperate letter:

> I came to town last night late with Lady Coull ... and ernestly hope it may
> be forgiven ... I have now been in the north these many months bypast,
> destitute of all support ... [I have come] to implore your parental affection
> and humbly beg you'll let me know to what scene of life you design me,
> that now when I am young I may take proper methods ... I have wrot many
> letters from the north to your lordship on this subject but unluckily I never
> had any return, and therefore I am now come inn my own person.

Somewhere, either at the school in Inverness or at his Aunt Coull's hands
Roderick had learnt to spell rather better than his father or the servants at
Tarbat could.

Earl John must have had a faint access of parental energy, for he kept a
letter from a friend in London with useful, if rather prosy, information
about the best foreign towns and Academies to which to send a Scottish
nobleman's son.

> Paris has good masters but very dear, and is full of diversions and of Scotch
> that were in the Rebellion (the 1715 and 1719 Risings) so that unless a man
> has a mind to declare himself an enemy to the present establishment it would
> be highly imprudent ... Angers has a good Riding Master, but the place is
> full of English and has no mathematikal or Italian masters worth a tack ...
> Louveins has a good academy ... a polite court

and so on round the protestant cities of Europe. Nothing apparently ever came of it for my lord's sons.

Where George was finally educated is not recorded: Roderick, however, was sent to a crammer's Academy in London, run by a Mr Watts and his brother, possibly a military academy. Rorie wrote to his elder brother George, who was in Edinburgh in July 1725 that

> yesterday finishing one half-year with Mr Watts I got up my account, went directly to Sir William Gordon believing he was to advance me money to clear it and supply me with other necessaries but he told me he had no orders for it, and to write to you. [Gordon had just finished marrying his daughter to George, Lord Tarbat, and did not feel wholly obliged to take on the expenses of the whole family, in their father's lifetime.] The sum of what is to pay for the six bypast months being £55 14. 6d. besides eleven guines to the Fencing Master for perfecting me ... by this time stocks beginn to turn low with me which I hope you cannot be surprised with, since I had the last from yourself half a year ago ... I wish you good journey and safe arrival in Ross-shire [15 July 1725]

In September of the same year Mr Watts wrote to Sir William Gordon announcing that he was expelling Mr Roderick Mackenzie 'who has behaved himself so irregularly and so inconsistently with the rules of our house and that there is no possibility of his staying with us'. He was sent into the Royal Navy, but transferred into the army and served in the Royal Dragoons. In 1724 his father and elder brother had executed a joint deed of gift 'for love and favour to Mr Rod. Mackenzie before five witnesses, to pay him £360 sterling. However, it was Gordon who paid, a year later, £300 to Roderick for 'all my charges for clothes, education and fitting out at sea', for which he gave receipt. He had no real grievance. In 1745 he was serving in Ireland and was then posted with his regiment to Flanders, so did not see service on behalf of King George in Scotland during the Forty-Five. Years after, shortly before he died, ex-Earl George accused Roderick of having betrayed him in the affray in front of Dunrobin Castle, but there is not a shred of evidence to support this, which one trusts was merely the bitterness of an old man seeking a focus for his misfortunes. Roderick married and had a son, also in the army, and on the death of Lord Macleod without children in 1789, this son Captain Kenneth Mackenzie inherited Tarbat House.

Patrick and William, the next pair of boys, were settled with a little help from Uncle Elibank and money from their eldest brother. Soon after George was married he sent the 'melancholy news of the death of his sister Mary' in June 1726 to their uncle Elibank at Ballancrieff. About William, Lord Elibank wrote in reply: 'I have not yet had ane opportunity to speak to Bailly Fall but I know that at your brother's entry to him there must be £100 Sterling payed down with him as Prentice fee', and until George had produced this sum—and do not forget it represented nearly two years rent from the whole barony of Coigach—Elibank was not prepared to bother the Baillie in Edinburgh. 'Your brother Mr William is just now here but', he went on austerely, 'it is impossible for him to see anybody till once you order mourning to him for his sister, for all *my family* are in mourning for her'. William soon after joined the Scotch-Dutch regiment in the Low Country, and transferred in 1737 to the East India Company's service. He was lost in a violent typhoon at sea off the coast of Bombay, on an expedition against the sea-chief Angria. Patrick, the fourth son to survive, was indeed indented to a merchant, whether Baillie Fall or another is not known. He went out to the West Indies, where he made and lost a fortune in the sugar trade in Jamaica. His eldest brother, in exile after the Forty-Five mentioned in a letter to his chamberlain Meddat in 1755 that his brother Peter was arrived from Jamaica, and had left a factor in London. The former Earl had hopes that Peter would be able to support the head of the family a little. Unfortunately, like so many sugar planters, Peter had evidently lived off advances given by Agents to his estates, and although he left an elaborate twenty-two page Will in 1773, there was nothing for any of his legatees. He had made his nephew John Lord MacLeod his chief legatee, willing him 'all his lands in Jamaica: the freehold estate of Flint River, and a leasehold called Tryall', out of which his sister Anne was to have £50 per annum, and other personal effects which included 'a considerable number of negroes'. The freehold of a property in Esher, Surrey, was to go to his companion, Mistress Barbara Heron, with £100 per annum. Unfortunately there was no prospect of any of these provisions being implemented. Tryall estates' lease expired in the year the Will was made and Peter was in debt to Messrs Mure Son, and Atkinson, his agents in London, for a large sum on balance of account, on which they held the mortgage for Flint River; and Richard Oswald Esq had lent 'about £2,000' for which he held the mortgage of the Esher property. Years later when Lord MacLeod was in Madras he wrote a business letter to a Mr Gardner in Calcutta, urging him to act in the matter of £2,500 still due to him from the Jamaica Estates of Peter Mackenzie: colonial business had become global, but in this case it was apparently not profitable.

Earl John had four more sons, including Gideon who died of whooping cough. Of the third family, James 'died young' of some other killing trouble not recorded; but Norman and Hugh both survived and, due to the help of MacLeod of MacLeod their half-brother, were both able to get commissions in the States-General's Scotch-Dutch regiments. Sir Norman MacLeod wrote from the House of Commons to Earl George in Edinburgh in 1741 that 'the House of Commons affords matter for no

7   William, the eldest son of the family of the third Earl and Bonnie Bel, died
at the age of seven soon after this curiously stiff picture was painted.

8 The three eldest children of the third Earl: John Lord MacLeod and the Ladies Isabella and Mary, painted about 1741. They were old Lord Lovat's pets.

amusement' and goes on to discuss foreign affairs: '... the Dutch are forming new companies: I had good reason to expect one for our brother Hugh but am disappointed'. Norman got a transfer to the British army in 1757, to Montgomerie's Highlanders, 78th of Line, and fought in America on the frontier against both Indians and Frenchmen. Neither married.

It is a relief to turn from the neglected family of the second Earl to the cherished offspring of the third. Their rooms were carefully furnished, their portraits were painted, with their parents and with pet dogs and garlands of flowers; their education was undertaken at home and in Edinburgh, and the girls had a spinnet to practise on in the schoolroom at Tarbat. Their uneventful childhood is not much recorded, except by glancing mention in letters of Lord Lovat's, until the disasters which followed the Jacobite Rising swept away all the happy life at New Tarbat. Two children had died, William born in 1735, died at the age of seven, and one daughter, merely a nameless note on a pedigree, must also have been an early casualty.

In 1742, when the elder children were in their mid-teens they were boarded in Edinburgh with the family lawyer, Leonard Urquhart, WS who supervised their education at the hands of the masters of Old Town. Urquhart sent a message at the end of a business letter that 'My Lord MacLeod and the young ladies are well'. Several letters from Lord Lovat, who was a much older relative of the Cromartie Mackenzies, are printed in Fraser's *History*. Lovat may have been an old humbug, as his enemies often declared, but he was an old charmer too, as they also conceded. In 1739 he promised to come over to Tarbat House with

> the triumphing sword of your great and worthy ancestor and my great grand-uncle Sir Rory, Tutor of Kintail. I design to cause brush it and dress it up, but I was advised by your friends and mine to keep it in the old rusty dress it is in till I put it in your lordship's hands.

It was designed as a present to young John, then about fourteen, who had become friendly with Lovat's own son. Was this a coded gesture? We must take it at face value without other evidence, though a curious circumstance has just come to light. In the 1980s a broadsword was bought by a collector of such things, and he has proved that it is the sword surrendered by the Earl at Dunrobin on 15 April 1746, to Ensign Mackay. It is a particularly elegant version of a Highland Broadsword, made by a famous swordsmith in Stirling, Patrick Murray. The hilt is embellished with delicate gold inlay, done probably in Edinburgh sometime between 1740 and 1745. The blade is contemporary, made in Solingen by one of the best German cutlers, but stamped, for the Scottish market, with the

spurious and sentimental name—'Andria Farara'—implying tradi-
tional good quality. Was it Lovat's gift of their ancestor's sword which
reminded Cromartie to be arming himself in case of need? Lovat's every
action needs to be scrutinised carefully; the sword episode looks like a
clever piece of covert recruiting for the Jacobite cause.

Lovat's correspondence was always flowery. In one letter he ends:

> I hope that this letter will find [you] and the worthy Countess and good
> Lady Bel and the other lovely ladies in perfect health ...

The old courtier: Lady Bel was only just into her teens, and her sisters a
good deal younger, and no doubt highly gratified to be noticed. He also
sends messages and compliments in each letter to 'My dear Lord MacLeod',
also a teenager, and to 'Lady Bel and the pretty family', even when (as
was generally the case) the real purpose of the letter was to ask a favour or
to relate some local news. Lovat's letters are the only source of information
about a dangerous illness that the Earl suffered in Dingwall in 1743, so
sudden and severe that the Countess rode to his side in the middle of the
night. Lovat congratulated him on his recovery, adding:

> I pray God preserve her Ladyship and you together for many years in perfect
> health: for as I believe you the handsomest couple in the world, so I believe
> you the happiest by the mutual love you have for one another, which must
> make the marriage bed comfortable.

Lovat, however, noted elsewhere that it was drinking bad wine in Dingwall which had brought on the illness. There seems no doubt of the regard
and close family links that united Cromartie and Lovat at this point,
proved later when together they raised regiments for the cause of Prince
Charles Edward Stuart.

After the defeat of the Jacobite army in April 1746 the break-up of the
family of Cromartie was complete and they never achieved unity again.
The Earl and his heir were taken prisoner outside Dunrobin Castle, on the
eve of the battle of Culloden, and were charged with the capital crime of
High Treason. They both pled guilty. One week after their removal in a
ship of the Royal Navy bound for the Tower of London, the Countess
obtained a pass from the victorious Duke of Cumberland's office in
Inverness, to go from Tarbat to join her husband:

> Permit by Sir Edward Fawkener in Favour of Isabella Countess of Cromartie
> and the Ladies Isabella, Mary and Anne Mackenzie, her daughters, their
> servants, equipage, horses etc, freely to go from hence to London by sea or
> by land as will best suit their conveniency. Given at Inverness by His Royal
> Highness' command, April 24 1746.

By this time Cromartie was in the Tower and her son John in a prison-hulk moored off Tilbury. The Countess left Isabella (then twenty) in charge of the other sisters in Edinburgh, staying with their lawyer Leonard Urquhart, and hurried south. She was accompanied only by a young ghillie lad, though she was later joined by her maid, Jean Murray. She left in Tarbat four younger children including George, the only other surviving son who, if his father and brother were beheaded would become the inheritor. He was aged between twelve and fourteen. Also there in the charge of Mistress Mackenzie of Meddat and their housemaids were the three youngest girls, the Ladies Jane, Amelia and Margaret, called Peggie. Peggie was only twelve months old, as we know from Lovat's flowery letter of congratulation to her parents in April 1745. She would still be occupying the 'wickerwork cradle' in the nursery, with perhaps her sister Amelia about a year older still in the 'wanscot cradle' of the Inventory. It was to be nearly ten years before Peggie was restored to her parents. Amelia they never saw again. Jane eventually joined her elder sisters in Edinburgh.

The correspondence between Meddat and his former master in the Tower of London was a very full one, conducted deferentially by Meddat, and with complete disregard for the circumstances the Earl continued to give him orders about the estate (which he had little hope of anyone carrying out), or to demand increasingly querulously that Meddat find him money from his former tenants and relations in the north. The Earl made several demands for the return of his daughters, when a suitable escort could be found, and Meddat apparently quite disregarded these requests. It seems that he and Mistress Meddat had become very fond of the little girls, and were loathe to give them up. The first mention is in a letter of 30 August 1746 written from 'The Toure of London', by Jean Murray, the personal maid of the Countess, to Mackenzie of Meddat about Master George. As John Lord Macleod was in the Tower of London under a charge of Treason as well as his father, it was important to the succession to make sure George was well cared-for. Mistress Murray wrote quite sharply:

> My Lady desyres me to writ to you both she and my lord are very surprised at your refusing to let Master Georgie go to Edinburgh when Lord and Lady Arneston desyred it, [Lady Arniston, a close relative of Countess Bella, had married Henry Dundas of Arniston, that rising and impeccably Hanoverian lawyer] for my lady sayes altho' she did no writ about it, you might be sure she uad approve of it ... Therefor her ladiship desyres he may be sent with the first opportunity, ether by sea or by land ... I understand from Edinburgh it hes given a good dell of offence, the refusing to send him, and my ladie says she's not at all surprised at it. My Lord and Ladie and Lord Mcleod and all the yong ladies is very uell ...

Few know my Face,tho'all Men do my Fame:
Look ſtrictly, & you'll quickly gueſs my Name:
Through Deſerts, Snows & Rain I made my Way,
My Life was daily riſqu'd to gain the Day! –
Glorious in Thought! but now my Hopes are gone;
Each Friend grows ſhy,— & I'm at laſt undone.

9　 The third Earl of Cromartie, in the dark days in the Tower, when this fly-
sheet was produced to emphasise his contrition for an Act of Treason in raising
a Regiment in Prince Charles' cause.

10 Bonnie Bel, Isabella Countess of Cromartie whose determined pleas in her husband's cause largely influenced the granting of his Pardon in 1748.

The date was 30 August, five months after the small children had been left at Tarbat. George went to Arniston to his aunt. The eldest daughter, Isabella, joined her parents.

Jean Murray, the maid, and John Mackenzie of Meddat continued to correspond. On 20 November 1746 Meddat wrote to her with news of the children.

> The young ladies at New Tarbat are all well. Lady Jean was dull for some days after Master Georgie went south but she was brought over here in the daytime, and the berns (bairns) diverted her. Lady Amelia dos not walk her lone as yett. She's able enufe if she was not afraed of a fall. She can walk by the wall out of the room till the back door of the house, without any assistance. and Lady Margrat goes round the whole dining room by a haill.

Meddat ends by sending 'four ankers butter packed ready to be sent by the first ship, and some honey' and discreetly wishing my lady 'a hapie hour', the first indication of her new pregnancy.

Three months later on 10 January 1747 Jean Murray wrote to Meddat again:

> Sir I received yours and wold have wrot befor nou, but still uas putting of till I should habe the agriable neus to writ you of my lady's safe deliverie, but as she is still on foot yet I send you this to know they are all well and in prity good spirites, in spite of the united mealice of ther enemies ... I am glad to hear the cheldren are all uell ...

In December of 1746 Leonard Urquhart wrote to Meddat to thank him for the 'Chist of Drawers for Lady Caroline's use, sent to Edinburgh ... Lady Carrie and Master George are very well ...'. News of the birth of the new baby in the Tower was still awaited by Meddat at end of January 1747. When the daughter was finally born she was reported (by popular gossip, not in the family papers) to bear a red birthmark round her neck, just where the headsman's axe would be expected to strike her father. She was given the good Hanoverian name of Augusta and was the last child of the family.

In March 1748 Cromartie was pardoned and released on condition he stayed in England. He was granted a pension of £200, and his estates annexed to the Crown in perpetuity. He and his son had pleaded guilty: the three other Scottish lords, Balmerino, Kilmarnock and old Lovat were executed. Soon after congratulating Cromartie on his release Meddat wrote a second letter, on 29 April 1748, with bad news of Amelia, then about four or five years old. 'Lady Aemelia has the pox. I sent for Dr Menzies to see her, and Robert Forbes the surgeon attends her close. The pox appeared last Saturday, she has not a great many of them'. Meddat went on to say that the child had had a fall a week before, and 'hart her thigh, and it swolled ... all the care possible is taken of her'. A week later Meddat wrote again

> I wrot your lordship that Lady Aemelia was Bad. She departed this life the 3rd [May] at 9 at night. Dr Menzies and Mr Forbes the surgeon had tolerably good hopes of her till she feavered in the Return of the Pox, the purple pox appeared on her; she was interred yesternight, a few friends present. The other two young ladies are prittie well.

They continued pretty well in spite of a terrible outbreak of small-pox in the neighbourhood. Meddat in a hardly tactful way continued to report casualties all round them. At the end of the month, Meddat sent his wife to Edinburgh with Lady Jeannie [Jane] and Cromartie suggested in his next letter that four year old Lady Peggie should move into Meddat's house from Tarbat: 'Now that Peggie is alone she will be better in your house ... its easie to figure the situation of an infant in a ghastly forsaken house with but a single maid'. It is fairly clear from Meddat's earlier letters that the child had been living at Meddat ever since her mother had left; there is no explanation why Mistress Meddat left Peggie behind when she took Jeannie to join her sisters. Cromartie continues to urge that the child is sent to join her family: Meddat blandly does not reply to those paragraphs, in any of the remaining letters. It seems clear that Meddat and his wife were very fond of the child.

In July 1748 the 'late' Earl wrote to Meddat about 'a small vessel of Gilbert Barclay's ... if that might be a safe vessel for Peggie as I wrote to you in my last, send her and her maid by the first occasion'. A month later Cromartie, now in Devon, wrote that he and his wife were 'unaisie' to have no word of Peggie and her maid, and that their forwarding agent was now Alexander Mackenzie, Oyleman in London. Meddat continued to write long and courteous letters about estate and financial matters. He stopped giving any news of Lady Peggie. Again in 1750 Cromartie wrote suggesting another reliable skipper, Captain Reid, whose ship the *Helen of Inverness* was expected to come to London River. Meddat appeared deaf to this request: however a letter seems to be missing. In the next Cromartie sounded quite querulous

> I have no doubt of Peggie's being well cared for where she is. As her sisters Caroline and Jeanny are to come here at the beginning of the summer it will be best to send her to Edinburgh in the spring that they may be able to come together.

He went on crossly that Meddat had sent some of the wrong things from Tarbat, and that Skipper Reid had not taken care: 'the looking-glasses

were all wet and spotty'. As Meddat was the only source of income sent down from the former estates and friends in the north to the impoverished Cromartie family, he was vitally necessary, and could perhaps feel impervious to orders about Peggie or anything else. It seems that Lady Peggie stayed on, with Meddat and Mistress Meddat, only rejoining her family in 1756, ten years after she had been left in her wickerwork cradle at Tarbat. There is no account of the reunion which may have been emotional and difficult. It is likely that Lady Peggie's first language would have been Gaelic, and that her sisters had quite forgotten how to speak it. Meddat spells her name as 'Peigie', the Gaelic form. In 1755 the exiles had settled in London, in Soho Square, after a short spell in Hammersmith which they found too far out of Town. News sent to Meddat included that:

> Lord McLeod was just setting out for Finland to a fort he has the honour to command ... George goes to a very good school that is near this place, he is to be boarded at £25 per annum, this is a great sum out of our small allowance but his education must not be neglected, he is so fine a child and I hope will be a good scholar.

By 1758 four of the girls, Caroline, Mary, Anne and Jane had gone to South Carolina to join relatives, where three remained for the rest of their lives, marrying well. In 1761 Cromartie wrote quite jauntily that his allowance had been increased from £200 to £400 'by the benevolence of the new King'; this was George III, who succeeded his grandfather in the previous year. In the same letter Cromartie wrote that he expected his 'son George back soon from America along with that Batt. of the Royal Scots to which he now belongs as an Ensign, which his Uncle Hugh was so kind as to purchase for him'. Uncle Hugh was a half-brother of Cromartie's, and of his father's last family, and a military man.

With the Earl's death in 1766, the long sequence of letters between him and Meddat ended. Meddat also was getting elderly. From a few letters which survive between Leonard Urquhart (who must have been elderly too) and Lord MacLeod, it is clear that the latter looked after his sisters. In 1770 MacLeod allowed £15 a quarter to each of them plus £40 per annum board to Lady Jane and Lady Caroline, then in South Carolina. Their second sister, Lady Mary had apparently a successful matrimonial career in Carolina, marrying successively first, in 1750 a Captain Clarke,

---

11   How close the third Earl came to losing his head is witnessed by this broadsheet, published in Holland ahead of the supposed executions of the four Jacobite Lords—Lovat, bottom left, Kilmarnock and Balmerino: Cromartie, the only one to be pardoned, is bottom right of this affecting but imaginary scene.

12   Isabella, Lady Elibank, the eldest daughter of the third Earl, who eventually
inherited the estates in 1796.

and on his death seven years later Mr Drayton, a Councillor in South Carolina, and finally John Ainslie Esq. Her next two sisters also each married twice in America, and Lady Jane, the only unmarried one, returned to Scotland at some unrecorded point. She outlived her generation, dying in Edinburgh some time after 1820, still in receipt of her pension. She was the subject of a factor's letter to the then owners of the estate, when she was so old that it was necessary for an explanation of her position to be made when he forwarded an apology for her request for some more money—she said, the factor reported, that she was so cold and hard-up that she had taken to her bed for some days. The agent thought it was lack of management on her part, but he sent her some additional money.

Back in 1770, the year in which her eldest brother was prosperous enough to make the first payments of this long-running allowance MacLeod expended £1,000 sterling on his brother George, almost certainly buying him his majority in the Royal Scots. Their eldest sister, Isabella, who had done 'the most menial tasks' for her exiled parents, remained in England with them, and did not marry until she was thirty-five, when she married a cousin, the 6th Lord Elibank. She outlived her brother John Lord MacLeod, and John's heir Kenneth Mackenzie, and so at the age of about seventy found herself mistress of the newly rebuilt Tarbat House, and all the estates: a strange homecoming. She remained mostly at the Lowland property of the Elibanks, though a few visits north are recorded, a few petitions to her from ancient retainers were handed personally to her, and she demanded a full list of the parishes of Ross over which she could claim to extend patronage. She sounds a little alarming.

Lady Peggy, it is pleasant to record, married young and apparently happily. Her husband was one of the most eminent of the Tobacco and Cotton lords of Glasgow, and Peggy was his second wife; it must have been a love-match for an impeccable elderly Whiggish merchant of Glasgow to marry a penniless young daughter of an ex-peer who had only just kept his head on his Jacobite shoulders. As Mrs John Glassford, Peggy was surrounded by the greatest comfort and elegance, with a fine mansion in Dugalston. Her portrait, surrounded by her family was in the Glasgow Peoples' Palace. Mr Glassford once sent a gift of 'a fine box of linens' to John in Sweden and he was certainly well-placed to look after his own wife.

Augusta, the Tower of London baby, also married well. She too was no charge on her brother. She married Sir William Murray of Ochtertyre in Perthshire, of the family who had befriended her brother George at the outset of his military career.

The Servants at Royston
and at Tarbat

The servants of the family must be considered as a whole, because it is not always possible to distinguish from entries for payments for a cook or a gardener whether the man worked in Tarbat or in Royston. The more senior servants and the personal ghillies went between the two establishments, as would the secretary, and the ladies' maids. There are few places where one can be sure of the full range of staff. In a sense all the northern estate tenants, and especially the small mealers and cottagers, and 'the scallags of my Lady' were estate servants, bound by degrees of servitude of a feudal sort to provide services on demand. Little detail survives on the written record, but the fact remains that the poor tenants not only had to provide rent in the shape of grain, but also services of quite an onerous sort. The former factor, Meddat, in 1755, gave a description on oath to the new factor, Forbes, about the services of Castle Leod. Tarbat, a more recent possession, was not quite so encumbered by medieval services. At Castle Leod:

> The tenants were always in use of labouring the Mains (farm) by tilling, dunging, harrowing and shearing and building and repairing the office houses, drawing of timber, carrying lime from Dingwall and their victual rent to the same ... and several small services about the family at Castle Leod.

This could have left them little time for their own farms. Peat cutting is not included in this list, but figures in many others.

One old lady, in 1755, kept her patch of land on the Heights of Achterneed, above Castle Leod, by providing a leet of peat each year. The leet was computed to be 60 loads of peat, in this context woman-loads, in a creel on her back, first cut, turned, dried, then loaded and stacked 12 feet square and six feet high at the Castle. Hens were kept by all as part of the rent and 'kaim hens'—hens specially for rent—were gathered in at the Candlemas rental, as were the baskets of eggs. As Candlemas falls on 2 February, a notoriously bad time in poultry-keeping circles, one wonders at the age of the eggs, and the plumpness of the kaim hens. It is no surprise that Scottish country-house cookery makes such play with soups made of lean boiling hens, like Cock o'leekie (with the luxury import of prunes), or Queen of Soups, which in David Hume's version begins 'Take six hens ...'.

Services (which were due from all tenants) included an unspecified number of days' work at the Mains farms and were always at the busiest time when the mealer would fain have been at his own ploughing or hay making. 'Leading the rent', that is conveying the sacks of grain paid as rental to the girnel or warehouse, and then to the ship was another compulsory service. The wedders of the flock were another form of rent in kind: a wedder is a year-old castrated lamb. Wedders were often pickled or smoked, as the English did with pork to make bacon. 'Mutton-hams' were much in demand. Pig-keeping was unknown on the Cromartie estates up to the end of the eighteenth century.

In 1755 there was a family of six fishermen who lived on the shore of New Tarbat with a cottage and boat provided who were obliged to stand by for any maritime ploys such as taking letters or stores across the Firth to and from Cromarty, or providing fish for the household. They only had to do a few days hay-making and shearing besides this, and to bring peats in for the kitchen. Their family name was Grieshach, which might be the Gaelic for 'gloomy', or might indicate a side-line in shoe-making.

The lady of the household traditionally supervised the dairy and the spinning of wool and flax by the maids. The first Lady Tarbat did a great deal more; she seems to have been highly competent. Here she is writing a letter, undated but probably in the summer of 1695, from Castle Leod to her husband at Royston. The spelling is modernised.

My Dear Love: I received the horses cows and all as you wrote. ... I am told there was a ship of great burden broke to pieces as she entered the Sutors (of Cromarty) which I wondered much at, loaded with iron and I know not what else. The men are all safe ... as soon as John Macleod come from the Highlands (Coigach) which was the very day I first heard of it I sent him there to see what truth there was in it, and to secure the anchor and rope ... when John returns I will send you a true account. I likewise sent him to see if any money could be had for meal, or anything else I had, for the little victual that you and I sold ... (has not yet been paid for.) ... and the little money I had I was always giving of it to the workmen. I had seven or eight that behoved to get payment every Saturday. Its true it was but little but many smalls make a great. There is a great deal of cheese for the new crop, a stone of cheese for a firlot of bere barley. This is as all my neighbours does, but I can get none sold at markets, for it gives small price, there is so great plenty this year.

The interest lies in the difficulty of running a great house—or one of any

size—on the edge of a barter economy. All the landlords took their rents
in grain victual, and calculated the stipends of ministers, the salaries of
schoolmasters and the fines of the Baillie Courts in units of grain. A
conversion table, the *Fiars Prices* was officially provided annually. The
actual problems of paying the workmen and of the glut of cheese bringing
down the purchase price is vivid. A letter from one of these workmen
complained about delays in his 'wagery'. Lady Tarbat had other problems
with them:

> Our work goes on but slowly. You know Montgomery is not over swift,
> but he is jogging on. [Lady Tarbat's spelling gives it even greater poignancy:
> 'Not ouer suift bot he is ioging on'] I hope it will shortly be ready. I am just
> going about to cut turf for laying on the greens. [This was roofing turf]
> Dason is doing on, and now that I have horses I hope something may be
> done, but slates is the thing that kill our horses, for carts will not go where
> the stones are. David is busy slating the turrets. I am only now waiting for
> a little more lime, which is very ill to be had.

Dason later complained in writing about the delay in payment.

It is worth remarking that both here and at Tarbat House there are
references to the use of carts, not in very general use, in Ross in the
seventeenth century. The general shortage of iron which made it worth
'securing the anchor and rope' of a wreck at a time when her husband
was Lord Register Clerk of Scotland is also remarkable. Cargoes of 'gads
of Iron' and of lime were sent up regularly from Leith in the ships bound
to collect the grain cargoes. Before leaving this single illuminating letter
from Lady Tarbat to her husband there was some real gossip:

> I hear Will Sinclair is married down in Tarbat with Anne Donaldson my
> woman. She went for this without taking leave and with child to him and
> stays with John to wash his linen and make his bed.

Will Sinclair must have been one of Lady Tarbat's own ghillies, as she
was a Sinclair born; however she told her husband not to pay him anything
without her signed warrant otherwise 'ill servants, and he *was* one, might
wrong masters in a great deal of money. I left no accounts unpayed or
tickets given, as James Lindsay knows and Anne Menzies'.

We hear of Will Sinclair and Anne Donaldson in the Poll Tax return
for Royston in 1694. Will was paid £54 Scots, so he was quite a highly
paid servant. Anna is listed among three lesser women servants. This Poll
Tax return is illuminating for the Royston household, and, as we have
just seen, the servants travelled north from Edinburgh with their masters

on occasion. It is worth quoting in full:

[Edinburgh: Scots pounds]
Old Kirk parish: Tarbat, George, Viscount; his lady; daughter Anna, a child. Menservants: Mr Alexander Williamson (Chaplain) at £120 George Mackenzie (butler) at £60 Kenneth Smith at £120, William Sinclair at £54. James Manners at £84, Alexander Williamson at £20, Nicholas Montgomery at £24, Murdoch M'lean at £20. Charles Ross a boy unpaid, the cook's man on the cook's fee, Malcolm M'Given at £4. Hugh Dunlop and David Paterson, two hinds on bolls, being about 9 bolls oats 2 firlots other victual James Brown, Gardner, and his two servants at £120. The tenants on the lands of Royston are Claud Wilson who labours about 4 chalder and ane half, and Robert Pillans who labours 5 chalder; women servants Mary Hellenly at £60 Anna Donaldson, Barbara Stevenson, Bettie Clerk each at £16. Lodger, the Lady Clackmannan whose husband is pollable.

With one unmarried daughter and one married but returned to the parental nest, it is surprising that there were not more women servants. Kenneth Smith may be the predecessor of Charles Kinross as secretary. Nicholas Montgomery we know from other sources was the cook; George Mackenzie the butler. At a guess James Manners was the groom. Wilson and Pillans (who 'labour the ground') were tenant farmers of the small but fertile plots of Mains of Royston that surrounded the house, and the two hinds, Dunlop and Patterson, were general labourers below the money economy—'on bolls'—but as they were in Edinburgh, their fee was of the comparative luxury of bolls of oats, not the harsher bolls of bere barley. Consideration of the gardeners is given in the chapter in gardens.

The most important servants of the estate were the Chamberlains, whose title changed to Factor in the eighteenth century. On them the whole responsibility for day to day running of the estates rested. The most onerous of these duties was the annual rent collection, and the forwarding of the money or bere barley collected. Leases, and the business of the small judicial Baron Baillie Courts fell to them, and also the payment of dues, taxes and stipends to Ministers and salaries of schoolmasters with which the estate was charged. Each of the baronies had a separate chamberlain.

The chamberlains we know most about are the Mackenzies of Meddat, the farm that lies next to the house of New Tarbat. Danioll Meddat handed in the only detailed set of estate accounts which have survived from the period of the building of New Tarbat; not only was he responsible for the payment of an army of masons and stonecutters and carters working on the house, together with a squarewright and some painters inside, the general running of the estate also went on, with the loading of the annual grain-ship and payment of the boatmen. Not actually in this account which is dated 1686, but a year or two before, a chamberlain noted that he had bought sacks (only he called them 'sarks') for bagging the grain, at 6 pence the dozen, from Dundee. If the chamberlain had forgotten to order sacks for bagging the whole of the years' grain rental would have been put at risk. Meddat also had charge of one copy of a most important copper vessel 'The Great Boll of Tarbat'. The original was kept in the parish church of Tarbat and was of immense antiquity: it was sent to Edinburgh to be repaired in 1707 and did not come back until 1712, when it was included in one of the two ships' cargoes, freighted with the furniture of Royston. The boll was the Scots standard of measurement of grain, like the English bushel, and rents were calculated by the boll, or by its lesser components, the firlot and lippie. The Scots Boll, Linlithgow measure, had been standardised by Act of Parliament at the beginning of the Restoration of King Charles II, in 1661. It is ironic to consider that Lord Tarbat, Sir George in those days, was almost certainly a member of that Parliament. Ironic because there is a certain amount of evidence to show that the Great Boll of Tarbat was considerably in excess of the standardised or Linlithgow measure laid down by law. The advantage of this to a merchant-laird taking in rents at the local Tarbat rate of about 620 pounds imperial to the boll, and selling to the market in Edinburgh at the official rate of bolls of 340 pounds imperial need not be underlined. It is often called the Great Boll of Tarbat, but the best evidence for its size comes from the end of the eighteenth century when a famine had struck in the lands administered by the benevolent Commissioners for Forfeited and Annexed Estates. They sent up a ship-load of grain and potatoes from Leith to Dingwall and were distressed and annoyed to hear from the local factor that there had been a near riot in the place, because the measurement of the relief given out (in firlots) was much less than 'the customary Firlot and Boll in use in Dingwall'. The Commissioners sent up a brass set of standard measures from Edinburgh in their next cargo of relief; no doubt the beneficiaries continued to murmur at the skimpy injustice of the King's measure.

According to an inventory of the house of Meddat, dated 1662, as well as being custodian of this all-important boll measure, Meddat had a series of locks for doors and chests, and a good stonebuilt house of two stories, with window-glass and shutters in all windows. This was advanced stuff for the small farmers of Ross in the 1660s. Mackenzies of Meddat continued to be the trusted advisors and sometimes formal chamberlains for the next 120 years, up to the third generation from Daniolls. John, when Master of Tarbat, wrote to his father urging that Meddat 'gets some favours from the estate', and the neighbouring farm of Blackhill got a tack (lease) in the first decade of the eighteenth century, when George Mackenzie was confirmed in possession with a new tack, in consequence of marrying Meddat's daughter. His descendents were still in possession at the end of the eighteenth century.

The Mackenzie of Meddat who is most clearly defined as a character is John Mackenzie, who was a young but trusted member of the third earl's establishment in the late 1730s. In 1741 there is a surviving letter to him from the third earl with rather trivial instructions that the whin bank at Tarbat must be cleared, and

> below the gairdiner's old house is to be paired (cleaned) and burnt as well as that where the saughs (willows) were planted. Let as many men be put to it as may be got. I'll expect to see it finished against I return, also that the second tabel room will be plastered and the bulwark finished, and get all the plaster lime for the back stairs of the dining room, at Castle Leod ... Let me hear from you once a week.

Cromartie was in Edinburgh at this time. Meddat's patience was to be tried much more highly. In 1746, after the collapse of the Rising in which his master had been so deeply concerned, Meddat was the only figure of authority in the Estate of Cromartie. The government had done little beyond declaring the estates of the Rebels to be forfeit, and immediately, on 4 May 1746, a rather casual inventory of the house of New Tarbat was taken by the impeccable Whig neighbour Munro of Teaninich. An Inverness lawyer, J Baillie, was nominally in charge of the estates from the aftermath of Culloden, but he was content to leave the daily administration in Meddat's hands. So, disconcertingly, it was the 'late' or 'former' Earl, now in the Tower of London who continued to send instruction to Meddat as if his authority was unchallenged. Meddat managed to satisfy both the new masters, the Commissioners for the Forfeited and Annexed Estates in the shape of their factor, Captain Forbes of New, and also his old master the third Earl who eventually was pardoned but banished from any return to Scotland. This could never have been easy.

Once the Commissioners got a grip of the estate they took a Judicial Rental in 1755, in which every member living on the estate had to declare under oath his relationship to the management, what rent he paid, and for how long. Meddat went along with the new Factor, Captain Forbes, to Coigach and to Strathpeffer as well as to his own barony of Tarbat, and endorsed or corrected the sworn statements of the tenantry. He did not know how many leats of peat used to be brought up to Castle Leod from one particular holding, but that was unusual. He knew most particulars. His new masters noted his reliability, and used him.

Meantime, in the interregnum before the Commissioners became at all secure in the saddle, Meddat had spirited away much of the valuable family possessions from Tarbat House and from Castle Leod. There is no documentary proof of this, no reference anywhere that we have discovered. The proof comes from two sides: first, from the Inventories of

New Tarbat and Castle Leod taken by the government, showing a decrease of astonishing proportions in the furnishings from the last, pre-1745 Inventar: secondly, how is it that the family still have charter-crests and the portraits of their ancestors? Meddat has always received credit in the Cromartie family for taking the valuables out of the houses of the third Earl, and sending them to the safe custody of the Countess's old home at Invergordon. His opposite number there, the Factor Gorrie, figures in much correspondence but always obliquely. 'Mistress Gorrie is verie well ...', that sort of thing. How Meddat corresponded with the Countess's ladies' maid, Jean Murray, who was with her in the Tower of London, and how he and Mistress Meddat contrived to keep the baby Lady Peggie like a child of their own until she was ten years old is told in the chapter on the children of the houses.

The other Factors who deserve to be mentioned are Norman McLeod, who served the second Earl well though apparently got little thanks, and an earlier chamberlain in the extreme eastern end of Tarbat parish, Alexander Merchant of Wilkhaven who flourished at the beginning of the eighteenth century. Robert Dunbar, who came in to the picture with the purchase of Cromarty, was a small laird on his own account, a responsible citizen, a notary and Sheriff-Depute and responsible for the all-important despatch of the annual bere barley harvest from the port of Cromarty. He has terrible handwriting, so it is difficult to follow the details of a great altercation between him and Danioll Mackenzie of Meddat. Each was clearly jealous of the other. The accusations were in regard to grain not delivered, loading times not kept, and irate skippers storming at doors. The annual shipment must have been times fraught with passions, and the moment when the skipper had completed 'a full lading' and got his clearance from the port within the stipulated 'ten weather-work days', and had received his perk of Capligan for himself and his crew of 'ane barril of ail and ane boll of oatmeal' must have been longed for by the harassed chamberlains of the Cromartie estate.

One other source of Dunbar's annoyance was the high-handed interference of the young second son, Sir Kenneth Mackenzie, endowed with the Cromarty property by Tarbat, his father, and inclined to 'meddle'— the chamberlain's word—in estate business. Kenneth and his elder brother John plotted to sell a whole year's crop of grain in the Low Country, on their own behalf. It had already been contracted by their father, and despatched to a Leith brewer so the arrival of a Dutch skipper in Cromarty holding Kenneth's order and demanding freight or payment gave Robert Dunbar real cause for complaint.

The second Earl had others besides Norman McLeod to do his rather wayward bidding. There was a family of Innes' who were based in Inverness, members of whom are described as 'My Lord's Doer', and there

13   Sir Kenneth Mackenzie of Cromarty, second son of the first Earl.

was a character called Rose of Broadly, or just Broadly who was entrusted with responsibilities by the Earl in 1720s when the estate was harassed with creditors claiming the rents. Broadly eventually set up as a merchant on his own in Cromarty, and did well, a substantial house still bears his name. The third Earl seemed content to rely entirely on Meddat. There were also family lawyers in the background, to whom application might be made by a chamberlain harassed by the Baron Baillie courts, or by the demands for the Crown rents, or for the payment of the Cess or the stipend to the ministers in the Earl's remit. On the whole the chamberlains managed these large and various charges with considerable efficiency.

Many of the staff are known only by a brief reference in a bill, or as a witness to an account, or as an entry in a list of wages paid. A few of these in each category should be noted.

The household was, as would be expected, headed by a butler, and these are dominant gentry in most households. There is however very little information to be gained about the Tarbat butlers. A shadowy figure, George Mackenzie, was butler at Royston. He was evidently to be trusted: he signs the Inventars and may well have written them, and his name occurs in the Poll Tax return. That is about all. From the evidence of our admittedly patchy records he does not seem to have received a regular salary. With the first name of George one could surmise that he was one of the many illegitimate grandsons of the house, but there is no proof of this. Mackenzies of Blackhill near Milton, and of Achnahaird in Coigach, used the first name George in several generations, otherwise it is an unusual name for the Highlands. Another man, J Paterson, was described as a butler, and his wife Anne worked for the Countess of Weymss. Anne could sign her name but her husband could not when they were paid off after the Countess's death. The staff who did the bidding of the second and third Countesses are almost unknown to us. No record of them has survived, except for the nurse Grizzel who took charge of the Tarbat nursery round about 1718, and the Factor or chamberlain Norman McLeod, who was definitely of distant kin to the earl. McLeod wrote quite a sycophantic letter asking for a job for his daughter in the Countess's household. This was in 1725, when he had served for years in his own most thankless office. The letter first deals with the disarming of the clans, and McLeod asks the Earl for a letter of authority to carry a pistol, 'as your Doer, else how can I go with your lordship's rents?' He goes on:

> I understood after parting with you that your lady wanted a woaman, hir woaman being got tender and not able to serbe. If her ladyship would please do my daughter the honour to take her to hir serbing, it would be a great honour doon her and I can promise for her probity and good nature and believe she may be capable also for the work both whyte and coloured, sewn and imbroder, to very good purpose …

Her washing of linen and dressmaking was also extolled and she had been some years with another household. It seems hard that such a faithful servant as McLeod had proved himself to be should have to grovel for a job for his daughter. He had also had hopes, a few years before, of launching his son Norman off to Edinburgh with young Lord Tarbat, who was going there after school in Inverness. McLeod wished for 'Normie' to go on being body servant to Lord Tarbat, but he had not had any money for the boy's attendance in Inverness, and while he could manage that, he did not think he could fit him out for Edinburgh:

> although I am able to maintain him in Inverness all this tyme in board and cloathing ... I'm not in condition to bestow (keep) on him, out of the country.

It is not clear whether either of the McLeod children got the jobs their father hoped for them.

About this time the affairs of the second Earl became so involved as to be impossible to follow, and he was more often in London or Edinburgh than back on his rack-rented property of Tarbat. His harassed agent Rose of Broadly wrote in 1722 of his great pleasure at the earl's promised return:

> Your lordship should gather your papers together that are dispersed and scattered in the agents and the lawyers hands of which I am afraid you have not got exact notes.

Broadly disagreed with the other agent and tacksman, Mackenzie of Inchcoulter, who had the tack of Castle Leod in the 1720s. Inchcoulter wrote in a highly aggrieved way that Broadly was inciting his tenants not to pay rent to him. Another piece of property, the Fishing of the Waters of Conan, which had brought in much revenue to the estate a generation earlier, was now reported to be run-down and dilapitated, and the lease of it argued between several of the Baillies of Inverness—Duff, Macintosh and Robertson. 'It is not well done'. It had apparently been promised at different times to all three, for repayment of debts. The marriage of the heir, Lord Tarbat was hailed as a great blessing. Among the papers dealing with the debt-ridden Earl John at his death in 1731 is a legal Deed of Cognition raised by John Davidson, servant. He was acting for himself and two women servants who had grievances: Eliza Strachan attended the Countess Dowager of Cromartie (John's widow) and Margaret Skeen attended the Lady Amelia and others, all his children. Eliza Strachan declared that she had been engaged in 1718 at £2 sterling a year, but had only had in thirteen years a total of £15, so she claimed was owed £50 sterling and £5 damages. This seems fine imaginative accounting.

Margaret Skeen the nurse-maid had worse grievance: she had served 'the
Lady Amelia his lordship's only daughter of the late marriage for the space
of three years on a fee of £3 sterling yearly from Whitsun', but she had
only had £1. 6s. 0d. sterling. She claimed £7. 14s. 0d. sterling and £1
damages. John Davidson had lent the Earl £84. 5s. 8½d. which was a
'just and lawful debt'. These servants were claiming against George and
Roderick, the two eldest sons of the deceased second Earl, his executors.

We have little knowledge of the running of the households of the third
Earl and Countess Bel. We know of Meddat's loyal service, and the name
of Lady Cromartie's maid Jean Murray, who went to the Tower of
London with her, and that there was a ghillie who rode with the Countess
from Tarbat all the way to London, after her husband had been taken
prisoner in April 1746. Jean Murray claimed her wages, £5 sterling a year,
for the three years spent in the Tower of London with her mistress and,
grudgingly, this was allowed by the Crown lawyers.

To end this section on the servants of the house of Cromartie, here is a
formal Petition from one Isabella Mack Learnan (her own spelling), widow
in Ardevell (Strathpeffer). The widow Mack Learnan had had a son who
had joined Lord MacLeod's regiment when he was first recruiting and at
the time of his joining 'Lord MacLeod made Mr MacKenzie of Corry
mark her own and her son's name in his pocket book, promising her land',
and now about thirty years later, she was claiming it from Lord MacLeod's
sister Lady Elibank. The date is about 1800–1805: the regiment was raised
in 1778 and recruitment went on for ten years thereafter. The petition is
an interesting blend both of formality and of the intimacy of an old family
servant, one whose father served under Earl John. No reply to this petition
has been traced.

The Petition begins in the customary way, in the third person:

> Your Petitioner was born at Castle Leod under your Ladieships grandfather
> [Earl John] whose parents served under him and his son Earl George for
> forty five years until their decease ... a few years after while Meddat had the
> Management, 1746–'54 I think. Your petitioner was married in my parents'
> lifetime [she] gave her First Born son whom she was deprived of then, and
> ever will be, to the Dear Lord MacLeod to whom she would give a thousand
> sons had she had them all, and her Blissing along, at the time he made Mr
> Mackenzie of Corry mark her own and her son's name in his Pocket Book,
> when he told your Petitioner she would never want a farm on the Estate of
> Cromartie while one of the Family existed, and if any of your Petitioners'
> family was alive and able to labour the same would get also, and now your
> Petitioner is both old and blind for these twenty-six years, and have two
> sons that shall keepe House with her and weell able to manage a farm and
> that your petitioner now hopes and expects your Ladieship will be pleased
> to perform the Deceased Lord MacLeod's promise as the Almighty was

pleased in His Goodness to spare your Ladieship in time to order the same which is the greatest pleasure to your Petitioner ... to see her two sons settled in before she Die, and your petitioner shall every pray that the Lord will receive your soul along with his saints in Glory ... Amen, Amen ... Isabell Mack Learnan

The date would be after 1798 when Lady Elibank inherited. There is no hint of why it had taken the worthy and industrious MacLennans nearly thirty years to claim the promised land: something is not quite right about this story, though the promises made on recruiting the young men of the estate do ring true, and Corry's black notebook is invoked as evidence by other claimants too.

The kind of relationship that this petition reveals was at once the strength and the weakness of this Highland estate. A tenantry ready to sacrifice their eldest sons at the young laird's call showed great and unforced devotion: the tenants also assumed that reciprocal obligations lay with equal weight on the laird and his household. Any new improvements or alterations in the running of the estate were only possible within these constraints, or by ignoring them to run a high risk of destroying the basis of estate management under the old patriarchal system. Land was the ambition of all, land subdivided into ever smaller plots, unviable for the tenant and unprofitable for the landlord. When the last of these ties of feudal obligation and of affection began to part in the early nineteenth century, the estates had shifted into the harsher modern world, eventually into a world where properties were determined by factors and accountants. The ancient bonds of loyalty, and that degree of mutual trust were inevitably eroded and lost, though slowly.

Love, Death and Physicians

Bound up with cookery recipes, interleaved with them, are a number of pre-scientific remedies, and some formal prescriptions for medicines of the seventeenth and early eighteenth centuries. Hardly any bear a date. The first Earl was interested in natural science and was a founder member of the Royal Society at the Restoration. His friend Robert Moray, with whom he escaped from Monck's army in the north in 1655, was the Royal Society's first Secretary, and Tarbat corresponded with other distinguished men of learning, such as Professor Saville, Professor Gregorie and Isaac Newton. The practitioners who banded together to form the Royal College of Physicians of Edinburgh in 1682 were almost all personal friends and frequent visitors to Royston. Sibbald probably consulted Tarbat in detail about the lay-out and planting of the Physicians' herb-garden on the sheltered old monastery garden site that now lies under platform ten of Waverley Station.

We thus can expect that the treatments prescribed for Tarbat himself, and for his family were up to date and in the forefront of current medical knowledge. It is therefore interesting to look at a group of remedies which were dated and prescribed in the last illness of Anne, Lady Tarbat, who died in 1699. It is fairly clear that she suffered cancer of the uterus, and that she was ill for a long time, and finally returned from Edinburgh to New Tarbat House where she died in October 1699. She had been under the care of Dr Archibald Stevenson in Edinburgh; his first surviving letters on her case are rather jaunty. On 6 July he wrote from Edinburgh to Tarbat House with an excuse for his delay in replying that can have given no consolation to the worried husband:

> My Lord—Being taken out of town immediately after I had the honour of yours, and kept at Dunebrissle many days attending My Lord Drumcairn's daughter (who died of a feaver the 26th day after she was brought to bed of a very livelie sonne), it was not possible for me to give your Lordship a return—with the bearer of yours. I have now sent for my lady, four doses of those pils which her Ladyship was wont to find doe well in her colicks, and which I earnestly wish may now doe as well, and if there be nothing else ... I am verie hopeful ...

A couple of weeks later Dr Stevenson's next letter is more grave, it is written in Edinburgh as a result of a consultation between himself, Dr Pitcairne and Tarbat's son, Mr James, at Royston 'anent My Lady's present state of health'. They had letters from Lord Tarbat and from her physicians in the North, now lost, describing her state and he wrote 'we did conclude with these physicians that her Ladyship's trouble is plainlie hysterick'. This diagnosis indicates uterine trouble more than 'hysteria', in the medical language of that day. Stevenson sends some emollient words, and some 'easie pils'; thankfully the practitioners decided against the strong purging and blooding that was often then prescribed. Stevenson suggests that she should taken the strengthening powders in a posset made of double sweet milk of a cow.

About six weeks later the second family practitioner and friend takes up the correspondence. Dr Archibald Pitcairne wrote to Viscount Tarbat:

> Since Dr. Stevenson is with my Lord Hume (and merry too, I hope, for no body is very sick there) I presume to give my opinion ...

Dr Stevenson clearly enjoyed his fashionable practice and in August was not too troubled about his patients. Dr Pitcairne took the case more seriously, advocating Peruvian bark (chinchona, quinine) and a dressing 'to be applied to the sore pairts made from clean flax, soaked with whites of egg and aquavitie with camphire ...' The clinical atmosphere is a little lost by his third suggestion, which is:

> My Lord if the pain continowes in one place, make a pultess of cow's dung, milk and chamomil flowers and apply, or cause bake a bannock ... this apply warm to the places.

On 2 September, three days later, Dr Pitcairne wrote to James Mackenzie

> I think it is fit to give steel ... It did extremely well with the President for a long ague.

The prescription for Syrup of Steel is among the collection. It is endorsed *Dr Lowder's Syrup of Steel for my wife*, in the handwriting of Lord Tarbat: iron filings were distilled with aquavitie, sugar and some spices, and added to 'a quart of *good* wine' and drunk by the small glassful. This decoction might have been vaguely helpful to cases of anaemia, but not for poor Lady Tarbat. It is good old medieval sympathetic medicine, in which the transference of properties figures: i.e. steel for strength. Fortunately, on the next page is the formula for Syrup of Opium. There are two more helpful and soothing letters from Dr Pitcairne, still Locum for Dr Stevenson 'who is not yet come to towne', but on 17 October the first of the letters of condolence is recorded, and a few days later an order is received in Edinburgh for 31 ells of good black broadcloth to be sent up to Tarbat. One letter as a sample: a few days before she died a letter of inquiry had been received from Colin Mackenzie, probably of Redcastle, inscribed Inverness; he wrote formally and piously 'wishing that this visitation will contribute verie much not only to her temporally but likewise to her eternal happiness ...'. She had been married for forty-three years.

Disconsolate widowers very often marry again. Five months after his wife's death Lord Tarbat was writing charming love-letters to the long widowed Margaret Countess of Wemyss. One light little note ends: 'Right honourable, yours, or else little better than nothing' and apparently quoting with wry approval a rude little rhyme current in Edinburgh.

> Thou sonsy aul carl, the world has not thy like
> For ladies fa' in love with thee, though thou be an auld tyke

He was, it must be owned, seventy years of age, but he alarmed a minor relation by entailing the lands of Loch Sline and castle of Ballone (which the cousin had occupied for a generation), on any son of his second marriage. The cousin was not displaced. It clearly was a happy marriage, though a sadly short one. There are only a few surviving letters from Margaret Countess of Wemyss and Cromartie to her husband, newly created an Earl by Queen Anne. One letter is a little arch: 'I shall be very carfull of your Pegie' meaning herself, and ending 'My dearest Heart, ... It is now neer 12 past o'cloak so I shall add noe more but I am unatterably, my dearest life Your oune M.W.'

The second marriage was an additional charge on the Cromartie estate, as the Wemyss money went to her son David. Cromartie lavished gifts on her. These included a silver dressing set, complete with bottles, looking-glasses and brushes, for which he paid a silversmith from London, called John Campbell, £61 sterling. Various other bills date from this period. There was one from a dressmaker:

For making a Black Padusoy Mantua	0. 8. 0
Buttons and loops for it	0. 1. 6.
Making the petticoat	0. 10. 0
For ferret for it	0. 2. 0
For shalloune to border it	0. 6. 0

The receipt is dated 8 December 1704 and is also a London Bill, payable in sterling which, it should be repeated, was at the rate of twelve Scots pounds to one of sterling.

'Ferret' or ermine was not the only fur the countess had. Earlier in that year another bill was paid to 'Francis Rich at Whytehall', for sables from Russia.

The Rt Hon The Countess of Wemyss Har Bill

One Rusche natural Sabel Tipp Tippet	10. 0. 0
One Sabel Muff for My Lord	2. 15. 0
One Sabel furd lining for a [coat?]	2. 10. 0
One pare of furd socks	
One piece of Swan skin	0. 5. 0

£15. 10. 0
Sterling

The expenses of being Secretary of State at the Court of Queen Anne must have been considerable. There was a large establishment of servants whose names come and go, being paid by the admirable Charles Kinross, secretary. There was the expense of a second-hand coach-and-four in London, costing the enormous sum of £150. This, as present-day purchasers of cars often arrange, was paid in instalments, but Matthew Lamb, Coachmaker did not hand over the coach until the money was all in his hand. This coach was 'Bought and refurbished as new'. There are bills for gloves, for books, and several for wigs, or 'To the Piriwigg Maker', and portraits were painted.

The Countess of Wemyss and Cromartie died in London of her long illness, which was called 'rheumatism' by her husband and son. Her physician was George Preston, Surgeon Major to HM's Forces, and it was he who handed over the coffined body of the Countess to Skipper Spencer for transportation from Whitehall to Leith Road on 6 June 1705. There is also an account for his medical services. The funeral of this Countess was a very splendid affair, judging from fragmentary accounts, such as the grandly inscribed bill from 'WE. Her Majesty's Trumpets (sic) under-subscribed', four of them, who claimed and received £448 Scots for 'the services done at the funeral of the Countess of Weymm'. There was a service in St Margaret's, Westminster, before the coffin left London, and a second was held in Edinburgh before her final internment in the Wemyss vault at Elcho. The mourning Earl left instructions that he wished to lie alongside her, but ten years later he was buried in Dingwall. Her coffin had an inscription cut on the lead by the curiously named Henery Antoninos, Wright Burgess of Edinburgh for £6, and there are many other sums disbursed for funeral expenses.

The Countess's death came at a time of great financial crisis in the family. John the Master of Tarbat's tailor and principal creditor, Robert

14   The opulent Lady Wemyss who became the second wife of George, the first
Earl of Cromartie. She died in 1704.

15 George, the first Earl, from a print made in 1692.

Blackwood, had come a threatening step nearer. A demand for 'byegone annual rents' (that is: interest only) amounting to £4,171 Scots, for which he got a bond of corroboration was dated ten years previously; now he renewed efforts to obtain payment. Blackwood was a tailor burgess, and possibly also a banker. Certainly John, and possibly his father also, was heavily indebted to him, a debt that hung on for years until Blackwood distrained on John, by then the second earl. This financial stringency shows a little in the settlements made after the Countess' death: her maid Eliz. Campbell got a year's fee, owing from 10 March 1703 to March 1704 in London, and 'a ticket' (of credit) for the next year, payable on her return to Scotland. At £7 sterling she was getting £84 Scots. Anne Scott was another London servant, getting £138 Scots for two years. However, only Anne Duncan, whose wages are unknown got a gift of

> 300 merks Scots at Martinmas next on my account ... It is a token far more due to my present circumstance than to my inclination, for her kind and dutiful attendance on my dearest wife, did merit.

As the bequest was dated 7 December 1705, 'Martinmas next' was not till the following October 1706, a date tied in with the payment of the estate rents of Coigach on which the whole elaborate superstructure of the Cromartie expenditure ultimately rested.

The Earl made a Mortification, by a Bond 'in token of respect for Margaret Countess of Wemyss and Cromartie', starting with a token payment of 100 merks, 'being a fund for a catechist for the benefit of the Colliers in the parish of Elcho'. Payments to this fund were continued during his lifetime. Finally he ordered from Josias Ibrack in London an Angel by way of memorial:

> An Angel in hard metal after the same pattern which is in St James' church over the font, the same biggness and shape, to be bronzed with brass powder.

It cost £10 sterling, with another 10 shillings for the box and packing. 'Gilding' or bronzing a lead statue with brass powder was a fairly common practice at that date. This memorial probably included a latin inscription, the composition of which perhaps gave the Earl some consolation.

Before the last funeral expenses had been paid the Earl had installed Mistress Frances Walker in Royston as his Convenient: she was apparently acknowledged by the family and by some at least of the Earl's personal friends, as there are letters with references to her. She accompanied him to London and was at Tarbat House when he died. Thereafter she married quite well, a Major in the army, and claimed a good deal of furniture from the Earl's youngest daughter who, from the crisp notes she made on the subject, was unlikely to have let her have more than her due.

A curious document, without a name on it, dates from 1707 or possibly late in 1706. It appears to have been taken down verbatim from a long rambling monologue of Earl George's, during a severe illness, on the subject of his ungrateful and debt-ridden son. Part of it is in direct speech, part in reported speech, and it may be the work of Charles Kinross, then his personal secretary. It is a long and painful document: Cromartie thought he was dying (he lived seven or eight years longer). It begins crisply enough with a list of eleven major creditors of his son John, here called Lord MacLeod. Besides Blackwood there are a number of MacKenzie creditors. The debts amounted to 'Four Score of Thousand merks and upward', very archaic accounting, but after listing those eleven 'who are going to raise legall dilligence both real and personal' against John he goes on in a practical vein,

> those who are not [yet] will certainly do the same immediately or else they will lose money ... only counting the principal sums it amounts to 85,000 merks so that during the Earl of Cromartie's lifetime the Lord MacLeod, his wife and family have not ane groat to live upon. And no wise man can lend him any, who doth not resolve to gift him the money. I secured him and his heirs in four score chalder of victuall rents yearly and two dwelling houses fully furnished better than any other in the North of Scotland ...

After a lot more repetitiously in this strain (making it sound like verbatim reporting) the earl went on:

> I had as much money as would have purchased May's land in Ross and Kilravock's land in the shirrifdom, which I was forced to dispone of to pay 10,000 merks for John's debt ... and now he's broken my family and disgraced himself ...

The old Earl considered his own end: 'I have but little to add to him after my death by reason of my debts and great misfortunes', then in one of the unpredictable moves into indirect reporting

> he had settled 70 chalder of victual on John, 30 to Kenneth and 20 to James and paid their daughters' tochers (dowries) ... and [all blamed on John again] now absolute pooverty will soon extinguish his nobilitie ... But thanks be to God we are of a holy Religion which which invites us to a glorious and everlasting Inheritance. And turning to his Brother who is present said again 'this is a short and sorry testament I am sorry to expose it to my son's dishonour but his ailings hath proclaimed it and it is my duty to vindicate my own reputation.'

The Earl recovered then, and compounded with some of the creditors. He was a chronic asthmatic, and had at least one other severe illness, in

1691, when he was in some political imbroilment as well; the vagueness of his symptoms may perhaps point to a diplomatic illness, and the warm congratulations on his recovery might apply to either bodily ills or a return to favour with King William.

His London doctor was a Dr Gordon, a friend and gossip as well as a physician. His first letter—a long one dated 1687—dates from King James's day. It is clear that he had been treating Lord Tarbat for 'an ague', probably a malarial fever. He begins by quoting in a pompous way from two authorities, one of whom Sir William Fraser, in printing this letter, has identified with one of the physicians of Salerno who treated King Richard I of England in the mid thirteenth century; the second a more contemporary Venetian doctor. After all this long preamble, and the advice to purge and vomit as much as possible (under doctors' orders) comes the sensible advice to take a large bolus (pill) of quinine, and to use a number of herbal ointments which may have smelt and felt soothing but do not seem to have contained any specific now recognised in medicine— marjoram, camomile and violets.

In 1691 Dr Gordon wrote again from London:

> I will be anxious till I know the condition of your health because of the unnaturalness and great inconstancie of the season ... I pray that you should drink good wine moderately but in a greater quantity than formerly, because of the unfriendliness of the airs. Mak up of your better wyne an Elixir proportionate. ... We have one advantage by the wet season that we are much freer than we wir of the French Pox and Scurvie ... I know your lordship is curious to know any extrodinar phenomena may fall out in my practice, which you well know.

In another letter Dr Gordon again advocates the use of quinine, one of the few efficacious drugs then available. His grasp of scientific medicine was a little tentative. 'French Pox', syphilis, is not much influenced by the weather.

A trusted Scots physician, Dr Forbes of Elgin, wrote in 1694 about the health of John Master of Tarbat, just home in the north after his troubles with the stabbed Frenchman in Leith and the disastrous tour in the Low Country with his first wife. He had evidently been seriously ill. Another letter headed 'Advices for the Master' advocated that he keep off the strong country spirit distilled locally, that is, aquavitae or whisky. Dr Forbes had met the Master at a funeral and 'observed most narrowly'.

John's leg was better, he opined, but he still suffered cramps and 'ffynds a heaviness and tension and wearieness in the calves of both legs, and frequent startings of the musculous flesh over all the body'. However alarming these symptoms sounded, Dr Forbes thought that recovery was certain, and he recommended a sojourn at either the Baths of Bath, in England, or Aix in Germany. John did in fact live another forty years, apparently without further ill health.

None other of the surviving prescriptions is linked by evidence to the first Earl. He seems only to have suffered a short terminal illness, and his retreat from State affairs in Edinburgh and London when he attained eighty was, according to gossip, in order to save money for his next foray south. However it seems that his friends did take his departure as something final, and there are a few quite poignant letters of farewell from Edinburgh friends. His step-son David Earl of Wemyss wrote, for example, on 11 July 1714, 'I'm obliged to acknowledge that I had rather doe anything as part with one I love ... I wish you happily at home ... and will endeavour to amuse myself with some hopes of your return'. On 4 August Earl George wrote a note to Baillie Robertson, of Inverness: 'I forgot in the last letter to intreat you to cause draw half a piece of the best claret and send it to me by the same boat that I may get it free of jumbling; as also four gallons of the best brandy'. Only a month later a letter from Edinburgh to the Earl of Mar in London begins, 'This place affords very little news ... The Earl of Cromartie died Friday last, universally regrated. Upon hearing of the Queen's death he shutt himself up in his closet for three hours, was very melancholy when he came out, went to bed and niver rose again'.

He was buried outside the parish church of Dingwall where his grand-father had also been buried. A tall obelisk marks the spot in what has now become a municipal car-park. From an examination of his bones in a marked lead coffin, which was made in the 1870s, he was a man of well over six feet tall.

The following scrappy document clearly refers to the funeral feast in the town of Dingwall: the first earl had died on 18 August, but a delayed funeral was quite customary.

An Inventar of what was necessary was given out be Andrew Tailor be order to be sent to Dingwall 17 September 1714.

4 Bolls malt
2 Bolls meale   [for brewing ale locally]
the cattle [?]
Three gilbering staans [stands for either the spits for roasting oxen, or for
    supporting the barrels: gilber = an instrument]
Two barralls and on hogshead
four ashet [dishes]
three large pleaters [platters]
eleven silver spoons
on dozen forks and knives
four silver salt sellers

five small candlesticks
on pair razors and on spitte [carving knives]
fifteen cane chears and a half dozen Russia leather chears
Two fflagons
Two [ceagers?]

Among the many letters of condolence (and we may be sure there were many more unrecorded) is one from Baillie Robertson of Inverness, who was clearly caught in the thick of some town politics at the time of the funeral.

> To John second Earl of Cromartie
> Nothing but a Spanish Inquisition or the equivalent, as we are present are trysted with, could hinder us to wait of your Lordship this night at New Tarbatt but if our tryall is over this night we shall pleas God meet your Lordship Tomorrow and doe ourselves the honnour To witness the Interrmet of yr. Noble and Worthy father one of the best friends our toun had. We are wt. much respect
> Thomas Robertson, JHW Duff, John Stewart,
> Alex Clark, Alexnd. Macintosh.
> Inverness 22 September

The funeral of the first Earl of Cromartie cost a year's rent, and the money was advanced by this same Baillie Robertson of Inverness. The second Earl had an imposing document drawn up, pledging

> for the more speedy payment of so just a Debt to have sold and disponed ... in favour of the said Thomas Robertson the ... numbers and quantity of eight hundred and fifty eight bolls bere, Merchant ware of the growth of our lands in the Barrownies of Castle Leod and New Tarbat ... for the present crop and year of God seventeen hundred and fourteen and payable to us by the several persons and tenants afternamed.

There followed a list of the principal tacksmen of the estates, and the assessment is a steep one judging by the average crops collected in previous seasons. By September, when the funeral took place, it would have been easy to assess the probable harvest of 1714.

The new Countess of Cromartie was Marie Murray, second wife of John, the second Earl. She was the mother of at least six children, including the heir George who so appealed to his grandfather that the whole estate was entailed on him, with his father only having a small life-rent. Only one letter written to Maria by John while still Master of Tarbat survives. It is dated *c.* 1701, and is sentimental to the point of being too saccharine for quotation at any length. John was making excuses for not writing before, for implying that his sisters were coming to stay *again*, and for failing to nail his father down to a family discussion

> but the publick concern (I mean the parliament) does so intyarely take up my father, that to attempt speaking to him of anie pryvat business were in vain ... I doubt my dear Mary uill be so just to your husband as to condemn your dear selfe for entertaining the least thought that would occasion a minute disquiet ... I doubt not my angel ...

There is little trace of her in the record after this effusion; she had a dreadful time in 1712 with the children all down with whooping cough which carried one or two of them off, and left her ill. The Inventars of Tarbat House hint at a poor grasp of household economy, and we know from other sources that her husband drank heavily and was deeply in debt. By 1717 there are a cluster of prescriptions from surgeon-apothecaries and doctors of Inverness, and a couple from a very smooth medical practitioner from one of the Spa waters: his writing makes it impossible to be sure which—Senarborrow? He has endorsed it correctly and formally: *Directions for the Noble Countess the Lady Cromartie at Senarborow Waters*, and the directions run to four pages detailing a strict regime of drinking the waters in increasing quantities up to nine or ten glasses a day, together with a strong purging and a light diet. She died soon after: we have not more information about her condition.

None of the sixty or seventy medical recipes or prescriptions seems to date from later than the beginning of the eighteenth century. There are however a number of curiosities amongst the collection, particularly some much older alchemical writings, including *A sovereign remedy of honey which cures all diseases*, a purge *Good against all kinds of surfiets*, and *Dr Gaskin's Powder* which contained powdered pearls and ambergris among a great profusion of herbs and spices. There is a nice gabble of words *Aremus: Aramus: Arebus: Aqulisq* in a *Remeide for the Byte of a Mad Dog*, to be written 'upon a quire of paper'. The paper was to be folded over a pound of butter and given to the dog to eat 'befir it be all mad'—rather difficult to judge. The words with their hint of arabic are very like other charm-curses recorded from early Tudor England. The material may have come from Tarbat's maternal grandfather, Sir George Erskine of Innerteil, who was reputed to have a great interest in alchemy. Some of his books and documents were presented to the new College of Physicians by Lord Tarbat in 1681.

Some of the remedies must date from the time of Lady Tarbat who married in 1654 and died, as we have seen, in 1699. None, however, are in her handwriting, and her spelling is so different from today's that I have modernised it whenever quoting from her, or from her sister in law, Lady

Seaforth, or from Tarbat's mother Lady Margaret Erskine. All of them wrote fluently but spelling was far from standardised in seventeenth century schoolrooms.

Writing from Castle Leod to her husband at Royston, perhaps in the summer of 1695 Lady Tarbat first outlines the work done on the estate and goes on

> I am only now waiting for a little more lime, which is very ill to be had, for John needs it for Tarbat, who is indeed a very good grieve, and becomed a very frugal man. To tell the truth there is little drunk in his house or mine—not that we want it to any that comes—but whey is very plentiful and when he stays with me he drinkes nothing but whey ... I brewed only once since you went. You know I had very good ale in the house which I bottled, and it keeps very well ... Once we drank a few bottles when my sister Seaforth came to dine with me with her chaplain and her brother-in-law.

This letter was written shortly after the deplorable affair in the tavern in Leith, and John was clearly on his best and most sober behaviour when with his mother. His ancient grandmother Lady Margaret wrote at about the same time to her son, giving him her legacy before she died (she was married before 1626, so she was undoubtedly old by 1690). Referring to John's escapade she says 'If it were not for the offending of God Almighty it would but trouble me little, for these things are inevitable when young men, and men in drink, quarrel together'. These are robust sentiments, a man had died as a result of the 'young men in drink'.

II

Tarbat House 1656–1784
The Building of New Tarbat

Since there are few traces left of the New Tarbat building, we are faced with the task of rebuilding an entire mansion in our minds' eye, furnishing it and planting the garden—with nothing more to go on than scraps of paper which have survived in random order. There is less difficulty in filling the building with its owners, their families, their servants, and their neighbours, for they have all left sufficient trace in the records.

In September 1678 when Sir George Mackenzie of Tarbat was once again restored to royal favour he obtained from King Charles II in Whitehall a Charter under the Great Seal which united all the lands he had inherited and later acquired into one Barony of Tarbat. The lands included his inheritance from his father and grandfather in the east of the parish of Tarbat together with the new lands of Milton, which he had bought, and Fearn Abbey, part of his wife's dowry. He had bought the lands of Milton from Walter Innes of Inverbreakie in 1656, good corn lands which had belonged to a line of Munros. They had left a ruinous castle and a fine burial-vault in Kilmuir Easter kirkyard, right up against the boundary of the lands of Ross of Balnagowan. The castle was sited on the raised beach-line facing the harbour of Cromarty, across the safe waters of the Cromarty Firth, and it provided a much better geographical base for a magnate expanding in Easter Ross than any the Mackenzies had previously held. The Royal Charter merely tidied up a shift in Sir George's power base from the remote parish of Tarbat, surrounded on three sides by stormy seas, to sheltered Milton, with a sea-channel fit for large boats at the gate, Delny Deep, within easy sailing of the Royal Burghs of Dingwall and Cromarty, and near to Tain where he also held Bishops' Feus. Long before the Charter made it official, George Mackenzie had set about making Milton his head house, which he renamed New Tarbat, as he took title from Tarbat. It is not certain how soon he actually began to build beside

16   New Tarbat House, surveyed in 1755 (Courtesy Scottish Record Office).

the old Munro castle but it must have been almost as soon as he got possession. His mother was living there two years after he bought it, but it could not have been comfortable then, nor for many years to come. The family were compulsive builders.

It seems at least possible that the overall design of New Tarbat house was the work of Sir George himself, as there exists a scribbled document in his handwriting, without a heading or date, which one can only surmise belongs to the Building of New Tarbat. After giving some measurements and calculations he wrote, starting from the top floor of the house downwards:

1st story	3 ells	42 feet wt in walls, and 3 ft to
2nd story	4 ,,	dry wall in gavell (gable) so in
3rd story	5 ,,	length 16 ells

To this add the (end?) gavels or rather the four gavels, viz. that at each end will be about 50 ells, or one ruad [sic: rood] and ninteen ell, in all 6 rood and 26 ells. A door for ye entry of 4 ft widd and 8 high and narrow windows of 2 ft broad and 5 high on each side of the door: all the rest of the windows for the 2 middle stories to be 3 ft widd ...

And so on for two pages, difficult stuff for any non-specialist to visualise. It should be remembered that Tarbat's daughter was married to Bruce of Clackmannan and Tarbat was a close acquaintance of Sir William Bruce, the leading gentleman-architect of the day. A man of parts in the baroque tradition might well be competent to be his own architect and in the absence of any evidence to the contrary Tarbat's major part in his house's design is an assumption to be entertained. Fortunately there exists a drawing of the House of New Tarbat, possibly executed in the 1750s for the Forfeited Estate Commissioners, and the original of a later confident Victorian lithograph in Fraser's *History* labelled New Tarbat House. There are certain problems of perspective in both drawings, but we are looking at a square building with a central block of three stories, and at each corner round turreted towers up to five stories, divided by small string-courses. It is very much in Sir William Bruce's manner at Holyrood Palace. We can safely assume that New Tarbat was in this style though we will come no nearer an exact likeness. From a much later reference we know that there was some of 'Munro's old wark' still standing; some stone may well have been reused. In 1727 the master mason Stronach had orders to take it down and build it up. Munro's castle was not on the identical site. There is a suggestion of haste in much of the surviving correspondence—of corners cut, as well as the perennial difficulty of importing enough lime, in order to present a fine building quickly. Munro's 'wark' was built in the early sixteenth century, when the Munros of Milton were allied to the

17 New Tarbat House in Victorian imagination: the garden not accurate as there was a gravel sweep and the lost statue of Cain and Abel before the great door.

Earl of Sutherland, and both were hostile to Ross of Balnagowan, hostile enough to build a provocative fortress within sight of Balnagowan's towers. In 1627 the Munro lands were bought by another neighbour, Sir Walter Innes of Inverbreakie, but it is unlikely that he lived there much, with a handsome castle of his own at Inverbreakie, now Invergordon), and with the accident to Milton reported in the Kalendar of Fearn: 'The 19 of May 1642, the house of Miltoun was brint negligentlie be ane keai's nest'—a fire started by a jackdaw's nest in a chimney. Fourteen years later Tarbat bought it, and began building his own mansion adjacent. It seems probable that at least one wing of the new house was made from the bones of the old one, for very early on he is roofing a part of it, and employing slaters, carpenters and glaziers, and chartering the services of a very skilled plasterer to work at Milton.

The earliest reference definitely related to house building is to the landing of deal planks of various sizes, to the then considerable value of £653. 6s. 8d. Scots, in a contract dated 1663. These may have been shipped from Sweden, as was the case in 1686. There are various other clues, bills for 'Glasser work at New Milton' in 1670, and three accounts for shipping deals, and for slating—work which could not have been done until the 'deals' were in place for sarking under the slates.

The masonry was probably in the capable hands of Alexander Stronach, a master mason who was the tenant of a small plot of Tarbat property at Dam Quarter and who built much for the magnates and burgers of Easter Ross, including the fine Tolbooth in Tain.

The proof of rooms ready for occupation and display comes from a contract in 1670 made on behalf of Tarbat by his brother, in London, with George Dangerfield, Plasterer, to go to the house of Milton within Ross to plaster ceilings 'conform to My Lord Hatoun's house'. Dangerfield had just completed the heavy swags of foliage plaster work in Sir William Bruce's new building at the royal palace of Holyrood in Edinburgh; Hatton was the brother of Lauderdale, and had also built a fine mansion in Fife at this point. No price is quoted, but the cost must have been heavy, and the effect magnificent. There is no further mention of the plastered ceilings until Thomas Pennant passed by in 1774, and noted 'the swallows flying in and out and making their nests in the fine plasterwork of a once-great mansion.' A hundred years before they must have looked lasting enough.

About the most interesting of the early fragments relating to the building of New Tarbat is a single sheet of accounts, sent by the factor, Daniol McKenzie of Meddat to Lord Tarbat at Roystoun, Edinburgh in 1686. From this long document it is clear that heavy expenses of building were still being incurred at New Tarbat. A slater, George Mackenzie, a carpenter, and 'James Dick, Master Mason in the house' and a glazier and painters are paid, so are 'masons hewing 300 of the number of squarestones' and quarriers for 'Winning' 760 pieces of squarestone, 1,600 loads of wallstones in Apidauld quarrie and 660 loads of stones, Cromertie side'. The reference to building in Cromarty is confusing until it is recalled that at the same time Lord Tarbat was constructing a fine Girnel-house at the harbour of Cromarty. The stump of this building still survives, and it proves to have been constructed of the same distinctive 'bacon-streaked' sandstone, with bands of yellow and pink, as the lowest courses and north wall of the present Tarbat House, all that now remains of the first New Tarbat. It is a fairly safe assumption that both came from the now worked-out stone quarry of Apidauld, on a site now deeply excavated for aggregate. This quarry is not much more than half a mile from New Tarbat, and the land slopes gently down to the house and beyond to the sea shore, where the two Cromartie boats of 50 tons burden transported the stone across the Firth. The account goes on to detail payment to Donald Miller, Wright for 'upholding six cart wayn and making all new except the wheels'—which are separately billed as blocked and cut in the woods of Amat, 'the timber of six pair of birk wheels, and for carriage of them to Tayne'. The next entry 'For twelve pairs birken railles bought at Inverness for uses of cart trams and wayne rants £4.10.0' is suggestive of a railed wagon-way, though far from positive proof. There was also '18 pair ordinar cart trammes bought at the same Mercat for the use of cart axletrees'. George Mackenzie, Carpenter was sent to both Inverness and the Woods of Amat to oversee these purchases.

The scene over which Daniol Mackenzie presided must have been as busy as an ants' nest, with all the artisans, carters and pynors—these last are the lowest form of labourer. Dan Mackenzie was responsible also for collecting the rent in bolls of bere barley and, fortunately perhaps, it was a good year, with 653 bolls from the tenants of farms, in a total of 1,382 bolls made up from 'feus, teynds, Tain, etc' which he does not detail. He paid (in bere) the Kings Due (the Crown Rents), and the bishop's due, the stipends of three ministers, some small local debts and a large mortification for the poor of Tarbat parish. He was able to ship by Skipper Stewart two loading of bere which totalled 1,028 bolls. The charter-party for this shipment has not survived, though one from 1683 was concluded with the same Alexander Stewart, Skipper of the *Amitie of Inverness* to make the round trip from Inverness to Dingwall, Cromarty roads and Leith, twice in that year. The quantity of his cargo in 1686 is not given, but he received £100 Scots. Dan Mackenzie also had to buy, shoe and maintain the horses used to draw the wains. Some horses were sent from Coigach, as in 1679 when five horses sent to New Milton were rated at 245 merks. Dan also paid £33. 6s. 8d. Scots for 'a Strathpeffer garron for the stone cart'. The two foremens' fees 'yt work for your lordships' horses in leading stone, Whitsunday 1686 to Mart. 1687' were £52.00 Scots. The use of horses, and indeed of wheels, in carts in Ross at this date is quite exceptional, at a period when the sled was in common use. No oxen figure in this set of accounts, though yokes of six pair were used in Tarbet for ploughing at least up to 1719, when there is a reference to it.

From all this detail, which took up four well-written pages, it is clear that Danioll Mackenzie was in a position of some authority. He is one of the Mackenzies of Meddat, usually just called Meddat. Danioll's sons served three generations of Tarbat as chamberlains with patient zeal: there is an account of them in the section on servants.

In the following year, on 16 January 1688, Tarbat wrote from Edinburgh to his son at Tarbat House:

> As to the building I find it very expensive both their and heir [he meant at Tarbat and at Royston] but to put the house of Tarbat to some period in its shell see what is to be done ther for provision of stone, and I shall send lyme. I expected that there was timber enough at Tarbat for jeasts [joists] and rooff and windowes; but now that much of that is gone [there had been a devastating gale, destroying timber], [calculate] what will be necessar for floor and rooff, and try if yee can be provided of all att home, ether be Ballnigowan Inercharron, or Alexander Ross, and at what rates.

He goes on to discuss the hazards of transporting wood, and the various sizes which it will be necessary to procure.

> Deals for sarking yee may have there, but I fear yee will not gett sufficient clean deals for flooring. ... I intend to box it all, at least the best part of it, with wanscott [panelling] and to make the windows sash, so that the timber for that must be provided from Holland, and I fear the carpenter from this. I likewise desyre to know as true a measure of the grounds, for yairds, avenues and orchards as can be, and as I write to you formerly.

Lord Tarbat goes on to arrange a private meeting in Fife with his son, who should not dare to appear in Edinburgh 'because your debts will trouble you here. It is not in my power to pay them because my owne stresses me above what I can'. The expense of constructing two major mansions at once must have been very great, especially as Tarbat makes it clear that he was prepared to send to Holland for cut timber for sash windows—well he might 'fear the carpenter' for the cost of this. The earliest sash windows in London were reputed to have been fitted at Ham House by the Duke of Lauderdale, a further clue that emulation of Lauderdale was one of Tarbat's driving forces. These sash windows must have been amongst the earliest in the Highlands, if not in Scotland.

In 1706 John wrote to his father in Edinburgh, and it sounds as if tradesmen were still at work:

> My wife only stayed [in the drawing room] till her bed-chamber and closet
> in the third storie was finished (I mean neu floored and lyned): so if your
> resolution of coming north this season hold, there's no doubt of your having
> accommodation, I mean the first or second apartment, which you please to
> choose, and the pavilion-room for your daughter ... ther's no necessity of
> yur going either to Castle Leod or Cromarty ... ther's more want of furniture
> than room in Tarbat but if a part of the furniture left at Castle Leod wer
> added to what is allreadie her, nothing would be wanting.

A strong hint.

In 1707 there was still discussion of wooden panelling in the parlour,
and it is clear that the whole house was not yet completed. By this date
management of the Tarbat affairs in the north was in the hands of MacLeod
of Cadboll, who bailed out the Master (and his father also, as he later
claimed), when their creditors were very pressing. Cadboll in exchange
took on himself the overseeing of the estates, and actually lived in Castle
Leod, for which he had a seven-year tack or lease, at this time. In the
course of a long letter on several topics he says to Tarbat, away in
Edinburgh in the aftermath of Union:

> In obedience to your commands I have written and sent to John Dick,
> Wright, to come to New Tarbat from Aberdeine, who is report verie good
> of his trade and has wrought to the Earles of Errol, Marishal and last at
> Panmuir House. I concerted with him that he should report to your lordship
> a schemey of what is necessarie to be done wt. the parlar ... what deals and
> other precepts it would require, what was formerly wrought and what
> wanscott and deals are left ... If your lordship shall not think it fitt to bargain
> wt him after perusing of his report he is only to have for his expenses coming
> and goeing ane ginea.

MacLeod ends rather defensively that he hopes to have the full contract
sent to him, if it is drawn up, 'that I may not forheirafter be blamed or
challenged therefor'.

The laird of Cadboll recommended John Dick very highly in 1707, for
new work under consideration at New Tarbat, evidently not knowing
that he or perhaps his father James worked there twenty years before.
Dick made a visit for which he claimed 'Cost, skaith, danger, interest and
expence'—it was never cheap to get an expert to visit the northern
Highlands. Eventually he, or a partner William Dick, did do quite a lot
more work, round about 1712; we have no details, only a series of bills
of increasing asperity, over the years 1714 to 1715, ending in a Horning
and a Poinding. Court orders for repayment were given in the Com-

missary Court of Beauly, at the instance of William Dick, Squarewright now of Inverness, against George Mackenzie of Blackhills and five other respected and major tenant-farmers on the Tarbat estate, for £300 Scots, and 50 bolls victual meal or bere of crop 1715, plus undisclosed amounts for the 'cost, skaith damage, etc'. Dick threatened to distrain the tenant-farmers, to 'avert, aprize, compell, poynd and distrenzie all and sundry corns, cattell, horse, nolt, sheep, insight plenishings (inside furnishings), soms of money and all either moveable goods'. It was standard legal phrasing, but was very threatening, and was intended to be. Tenant farmers, however well disposed towards the big house were liable to be disenchanted when the creditors distrained on their possessions and stock, for debts incurred by the earl. No more is heard, so William Dick probably was paid at last.

There is little trace of expenditure on the house or the furnishings of New Tarbat from the time of the old Earl's death in 1714 up to the time of marriage of his grandson in 1725, and it is clear that John, the second Earl, spent as much time as he could in Edinburgh or in London. It is also clear from the slightly desperate note that often creeps into the letters of his men-of-business on the spot, in Tarbat or Strathpeffer, that he never answered letters if he could avoid it. Surviving papers, however, are thin for this period.

When George Lord MacLeod, the heir, married the Gordon heiress in 1725 he evidently moved into New Tarbat House and his father went to Castle Leod where he died five years later. The young couple also lived at Ballone castle on the extreme tip of the Tarbat peninsula. Their first son was born there in 1727, very much in the home of his ancestors, but a home which could not have been comfortable; the house had become ruinous and was soon after downgraded to farm uses. Young Lord John, the baby, was christened in water from the holy well of Saint Rule who was said to have landed on that coast and to have thrown a splinter from the True Cross into the well, about a thousand years before. At least that was the tale told by old Kirsty Bheag, 'a local witch', when the baby was baptised. Part of the surrounding lands, those not wadset to MacLeod of Cadboll, went at the time of this marriage to Sir William Gordon in exchange for ready cash to settle the most pressing of family obligations. One of the first things that George did on coming of age was to send for the Stronach of the day to put in hand repairs and improvements to both house and grounds at New Tarbat. Alexander Stronach, the second or even the third mason of that name, was an elder of Tarbat kirk, and a well-known tradesman. The characteristic work of the Stronach masons is still recognisable in many late seventeenth and early eighteenth century buildings in Easter Ross. They were tenants of the Mill Dam, or the Dam Quarter in Tarbat, and had built the pier and harbour wall of

18   The Cromarty Firth from the gardens of New Tarbat House, with the burgh of Cromarty across the water, about 1820.

Portmahomack for Lord Tarbat, and had sustained a pretty brisk altercation with him over payment too. Stronach complained, and the
chamberlain Alex Merchant of Wilkhaven concurred, that payment had
been promised in luxury bolls of oatmeal, but had been paid late, reluctantly and in very ordinary bolls of bere barley. Stronach had workmen
depending on him, he complained. This was back in 1699.

After the Forty-five, when the mansion house was annexed along with
the rest of the Estates, it is clear that it was an embarrassment to the new
Factor, Captain Forbes. The house in theory still sheltered the youngest
children of the 'late' Earl, although they seem to have been moved at once
into Meddat's own house nearby. Nothing was allowed in the estimates
for the fabric of New Tarbat, which is mentioned occasionally in a
perfunctory way. The rones were blocked, the tenants were breaking in.
Eventually an attempt was made to use some of the rooms to girnel the
barley, as there was no formal girnel house in New Tarbat. One was later
built, nearer to the mill which was in the hands of generations of millers
named Ross. Alex Shaw, the linen factor of Perth, tried to have a proto-
factory in Tarbat House, collecting as many spinning girls as he could to
work and be instructed there, but that did not prosper either. A reliable
tenant was at last found for the home farm which included living quarters
in a part of the mansion. This was a Captain John Mackenzie of Avoch,
whose relative was the first white man to cross the mainland of Canada.
By the time John Lord MacLeod inherited New Tarbat in 1784 that style
of building was completely out of favour; the heavy towers and many
rooms were considered 'gothick' in an uncomplimentary sense, and the
building was pulled down to make room for the smart new classical
mansionhouse of James M'Cleran. He did, it now seems, make use of
some of the walls of the old New Tarbat, which first decay and now
repair are disclosing, as the fine sand stucco of the north face peels off. In
the stable, behind the wooden panelling of the loose box at the corner,
there has been found a fireplace, built across the angle of the room, in a
manner exactly like Royston, or for that matter like Ham House in
Richmond. Perhaps it used to be equipped with one of the brass 'shoffels
and pokker' of the earliest Inventar.

The Furnishings of New Tarbat

Ironically, we can get the best picture of the furnishings of both Royston House and New Tarbat from the *Inventar of goods sent north* by the Earl on his retirement from public life in 1712. The 'plenishings' must have been the cream of his collection, and the list repays careful reading. The Earl added to the furniture already at Tarbat—of which we have no earlier list—such choice items from Royston as several four-poster beds, one new, with red velvet hangings which were the height of fashion. One bed was probably the same as his green state bed in Holyrood in the 1670s, and each bed had an accompanying quantity of bedding which was listed and used as wrapping for fragile and delicate pieces. There is an 'Indian' cabinet, a 'Glass cabinet with all belonging to it' and 'a Japan cabinet' with a separate frame carefully boxed and wrapped. There are several other articles which were also of Japanese lacquer-work. These chests were the most highly prized furniture of the age, imported from China or Japan by the Dutch and raised to a convenient height by a carved and gilded baroque frame of softwood made in Europe. Only a few survive. The frames are especially perishable. There are examples still at Ham House and at Dyrham, the mansions built by Tarbat's contemporaries and friends Lauderdale and John Werfen, secretary to the Duke of York. The other Japan-ware was a looking glass and frame, tea table and 'the little foulding black Japan table'. There is 'The Great Easie Chair'—for the master's own use we cannot doubt—and nearly three dozen other chairs, mostly with upholstered seats, some of green velvet, some of stamped Spanish leather, and six 'Jappan chairs' in paired bundles, 'wanting the covers'. These were probably a European attempt to copy Japanese lacquer, applied to a chair, a piece of furniture not then used in Japan. There are several boxes of candle-sconces, gilt and glass, one lot mysteriously wrapped in 'three fishing nets'; several looking-glasses of some grandeur, one with its own gilt sconces, two 'very large' glasses and one described as 'The Union Glass'. There are several tapestries—'Arras'; four of them travelled north in a cask wrapped round in a 'feather bed'. There is statuary for the house and the garden; 'Cain and Abel in a large box', and other things, including a mysterious little box with 'Two Rabbets'—were these carved, or the live progenitors of Ross-shire's worst agricultural pest? There is walnutwood furniture—a desk, a table, a cabinet and there is the 'large box with the clock'. One can only speculate on it being a long-case bought in the heyday of fine Restoration clockmakers. There are many bundles of pictures, maps and prints, of unspecified subjects; and china, glass and pewter household and ornamental vessels in boxes and chests. There are four screens and two boxes of window glass, and some practical sundries, such as two 'garding spades', a hogshead of Lisbon wine and a half hogshead of brandy. The list ends with '16 lasts and two barrels'—that is a total of 196 barrels—'full with salt', and finally 'A coach and six', with harness, spare window-glasses and all. No wonder Skipper Morison jibbed at the size of the cargo.

A particular Inventar of the goods sent north in John Morison's ship 4th October 1712. [Part only]

A large box with the head of THE IRON GATE
1 Ditto with the figure of CAIN AND ABEL
One box with a NEPHINE [statue of a nymph or Neptune?]
A large box with the NEW VELVET BED four pairs new english blankets twa down pillows ... etc. and all the Corniches (cornices) inner and outer bands, with the iron rods and the timber rods, and other several nails belonging to the bed.
A large box with the twa large PEIR GLASSES and a pr. of old blankets.
(Five other boxes containing glasses, dressing glasses, and *GLASS SCONCES* with gilded frames, some wrapped in English blankets, and 'a little BOX WITH CHAINY' [China])
4 GLASS PICTURES and a copper japanned coffee pot and lamp
A little box with two RABBETS
The matted bundle with a TABLE
A large box with the GLASS CABINET wt all belonging to it one JAPAN WOODEN BOWL and cover with the bolster and one pillow of the little other closet bed ... (and many other specified soft goods, used as wrapping).
A large box with the INDIAN CABINET and a pair of narrow Scots blankets.
One large box with the gilded frame of the JAPPAN CABINET and [apparently packed inside the framework] ane old English blanket, THE PEUTER MACHINE [?] with all belonging to it, eleven peuter trenchers, six NEW BRASS LOCKS, with six keys and two passkeys to the said locks, 2 large dishcovers ... and the little bed of the closet.
A Large Box with six pieces of ARRAS, the JAPANESE TABLE and frames, the frame of the INLAID TABLE, the little foulding black JAPAN TABLE and frame, four glass sconces and three fishing nets.
A matted bundle with the MALT MILL to Alex Merchant
A large chist with the old RED VELVET BED [bedding etc ...] and the damask cushions of the GREAT EASIE CHAIR.

A large box wt. THE CLOCK.

A box with the JAPPAN LOOKING GLASS and TWO GILDED SCONCES and an old pr. of Scotts blankets.

THE BOLL OF TARBAT.

A large cask with a feather bed and 4 pieces of ARRAS.

A little box with the figure of NEPTUNE.

A canvas-bottom bedstead belonging to the new velvet bed.

Twa garding SPADES

2 boxes with WINDOW GLASS

1 box with TWO SKRENES

1 box with TWO SKRENES

1 box with ONE SKRENE

A box with the FIELD BED

The bedstead of the old velvet bed, the wooden rods of ditto.

7 boxes with PICTURES AND MAPS

1 box with PEWTER

2 boxes PICTURES and PRINTS

A large box with a WALNUTWOOD DESK, slip covers for chairs

A fine LOCK AND KEY etc. [sic]

On box with the little INLAID LOOKING GLASS

A matt bundle with the head of the INLAID TABLE

The frame of a CLOSE-STOOL

A box with my lord's DRINKING PEWTER

A matt bundle with 2 BRASS HEARTHS

a box with PRINTS and 6 cushins

a large OVAL TABLE

A bundle of FRAMES for pictures

6 Bundles of old velvet chairs, 12 in no.

4 Bundles of old velvet chairs, black, 8 in no.

6 Jappan wanting the [?] covers, 3 bundles

6 Bundles of CHAIRS, 12 in No.

4 Bundles of new velvet CHAIRS, 8 in no.

One silk EASY CHAIR, one bundle

Two bundles of CHAIRS, 4 in no.

1 Hogshead of LISBON WINE and a half hogshead of BRANDY

16 lasts and 2 BARRELS of herring and salmond casks full with salt.

A COACH AND SIX, harnish and bridles, butt the harnish and bridles not being complete.

A box with four GLASSES two of which belong to the sd. coach and other two being spare: these sent in David Sibbald's ship and accept the same sent north by my Lord.

Endorsed on the back 'Inventar of the Goods sent North in Morison's ship, 1712 and David Sibbald's ship'.

The first full inventory of the contents of Tarbat House that has survived is dated 1719, and is a very full one, not all of which is quoted here, but the position of some identifiable pieces which came up from Royston in 1712 are noted, as are the names of the principal rooms still found necessary at a time when money was short but prestige was still riding high.

The house had a state apartment, the 'Shewed Rooms' on the first floor, corresponding to the Italian 'piano nobili'. A grand staircase led to these rooms from a marble floored anteroom.

There is a *Drawing Room* above stairs, evidently used as a best bedroom as it contained a 'Moyhair bed' and all its curtains and bedding, and 'a dozen chairs with fryed (fringed) bottoms and green stripes', a chamber pot and close-stool, and a bed for a servant.

The *Painted Bedchamber* was much the same, with a bed 'with stripped curtains, and a walnut-tree cabinet', probably a Royston one, and the usual furnishings. In the 'closet of the same' were stored some curious things: 'one table, one Bigg Trunk, 1 clogback trunk, 1 bigg case with 13 glasses, 9 broken, one timber box, another do. a table, 12 bottles of Rosewater, 3 Spearmint, 2 of Hyssop and another Deal with a little soap. One begins to doubt if the current countess was a very conscientious housewife.

Another bedroom has similar fittings, and both a closet and a room off it, one containing a bed with 'green hangings, 3 pr. torn blankets, a square wanscot table and broken sided chaise, broken caine chairs'. In the 'dark closet: the stumps of a bed, 1 red rugg'.

The schoolroom has a similar rather basic quality in the bare bones of the Inventar: It contained '1 bed of blew cloth, and silk fringe', and bedding; 'one chamber pot and 1 pair of tongs'. Nothing else is listed: in the next *Nurserie Room* there is only 'one old bed, Musselboro' stuff, tartan quilt'. Stuffed into another wardrobe (perhaps a later age would have called it the housemaids' pantry), were 'five hair besoms (brushes), candlesticks and candle-boxes, ane candle-fatt and a pr. of snuffers ... one yarn-winder (—) and blades 2 Great Wheels and 2 Meikle wheels, one pr. of Tow harns, 2 pr. woll shizors ...'

Evidently the countess did not keep her maids at spinning or the equipment would have been more accessible. It was for both linen and wool spinning, as the two sizes of wheel, tow hanks and the wool scissors show.

Next in this Inventar is the *Great Roome*, which sadly seems to have been a dump for the shipment from Royston years before. It contained, among other items, a red leather trunk containing '45 pieces of sewed slipps, curtains, embroidery, callico, etc.' and a large chist containing '11 green sllipt covers and the mourning furniture of two rooms'. (It was advisable to have this ready in case of need.) Then there comes a list which is rather sad, of the 'custom plaids' of four years' rental from Coigach, in bundles unused and unsold: '1 chist containing 10 pr. of blankets of Customary dues of 1716'; the same again of 1717; eleven plaids of 1718;

and the plaids of 1719; also more of plaids formerly in use, 20, and eleven English blankets, 2 pr. tartan blankets and one old silk twilt.' It is typical of the lack of grip of the second Earl and his advisers that no one had sold these fine white plaids as his father had done. They represented the rental of many acres in Coigach; possibly no one exerted themselves (except the tenants who spun and wove them) because the rental of Coigach was due to the Earl's son George, under old Earl George's Will. The rest of the room was taken up with a litter of boxes, containing beds and hangings, pictures:

> a great box contains 4 pieces of carpet, 13 of Arras hangings, 4 damask cushions of the Easie chairs, with 16 small pieces of the said chairs ... two halves of a furred gown and one coach-glass entire and two brock, 33 prints in black frames, 20 pictures in great gilt frames, 1 picture of ye. Chevalier in a Jappannes frame ... a box containing glasses, unopened.

The picture of the Chevalier would have been of James III, Chevalier du Saint Georges, a highly treasonable picture to have in the lumber room in 1719, but had cousin Seaforth been more successful with his expedition with Marshall Keith and the Spanish soldiers in that year, it would have been useful to have had such a picture to dust down and hang out again. However Seaforth was defeated by the Hanoverian forces in Glen Sheil, and went in to exile in 1719.

The apparent junk continues in a depressing list, all stored in the Great Room: '... 8 black velvet embroidered chairs 7 japanned chairs [twelve had been delivered in 1712] a postillion's coat, and a box with marble and lead pipes [which may have been for the 'water engine' or fountain that old Tarbat had hoped to install in the garden] and a small box with a snaffle and two colt-halters, and several small things in the window not inventared'.

The list ends with the *Outer Hall* which sounds unwelcoming, it just contained 'one cistern, one menteith, two shew tables without frames, 4 flour potts and two little stools, 3 wanscot and one fir table repairing'.

In the following year, 1720, the same handwriting records *In the Dyning Room Closet of China*, a very long list of two and a half closely written pages from which only a few items are noted here. It is only a guess that the first Earl had purchased some of the early export ware of China from Holland:

> Six blew and white sources [saucers] China, and 5 cupps of fine china, black jappaned cups.
> 32 blew and white trenchers, 16 white do.
> 12 delft dish blew and white
> 1 flower pott
> 1 coffee mill

1 lignum vitae pestal and mortar
2 copper chocolate potts and 1 smaller
4 Talidories with black frames
2 wt. gilt frames
3 Alabaster boxes
1 do. with broken china
4 Norse beer glasses
2 do. do. do.
3 vinegar cruet
4 sillabub glasses, 3 broken do.
2 German glasses with covers
2 bird-cage glasses
12 brazen shapes for desserts [i.e., jelly moulds]
2 warming pans, 1 bedpan

The list goes on rather dismally: '... a large brass candlestick 1 hearth besom, two whisks, ane broken snuffers ... 1 earthen jar full of honey, 10 milk coggs, 1 large cann of virgin honey, 14 pieces of sewing on canvas for chairs, 2 doz. damask table napkins, 8 Dornich [sic] tablecloths ... a large chist with foul honey for the bees in winter.' This list cannot have been made by any diligent housewife, and the keeping of honey and a bedpan among the good china and the damask was surely a mistake. The kitchen inventory was badly-listed and very short, consisting only of many bottles, flagons, and candlesticks, and 'one gird for baking and one baking-bread shovel'. It could not have been a comfortable house to stay in.

The next Inventar was taken by Hugh Munro of Teaninich at the order of the Government on 4 May 1746, three weeks after the Earl had been taken prisoner and the Prince's army had suffered defeat at Culloden. Munro, who supported King George, would have been a former visitor, and near neighbour. He enlisted the help of Mistress Meddat to make his Inventar; we may be sure that it represents the most accurate picture we will get of the interior of New Tarbat House under the care of Bonny Bel, Countess of Cromartie.

Her husband had inherited in 1731, though he took possession of New Tarbat House on his marriage in 1725. The House must then have been as neglected as the rest of the second Earl's affairs. The Countess had thoroughly cleaned and modernised it with new curtains and fresh hangings, with Georgian mahogany as well as the walnut of Queen Anne's day from Royston. There is a spare room which sounds delightful, with 'A standing bed with blew scattin embroidered hangings lained wt. a white silk damask ... 6 chairs all covered with the sattin of the bed, a jappanned table, and looking glass, japanned'. In the adjoining closet, was a 'Tent bed with blue-silver stuff hangings, the same with the blew room; one chair, a convenience, a grate, a screne.' The 'Shewed Room' had 'two standing beds, one with green Turkey hangings [was this still the green-hung bed with the Tourdeloos from Holyrood mentioned in 1678?], A yellow silk roof and bolster-piece quilted, the tother with a pale Camblett with a dark satin linen [lining] wt bolter-pieces and roof quilted the samen', and a full complement of bedding for each; 'chairs in flys [covers] of a green and yellow stuff, a finere (Veneer) table, a looking glass and a fineared frame, a gilt leather screen.' All these furnishings have been mentioned before, perhaps even the chairs of green striped stuff. Lady Cromartie had a young family and they seem to have been better provided for than the previous Earl's large brood. '*In the Narserie*: A little bed with blew hangings, a table, a screne, a wicker-work and a wanscot cradle'. In the closet was 'a chest of drawers a table wt. 2 drawers, a long wanscot box, a chist and an old arm chair'. The family were growing up. MacLeod had an ideal room for an eighteen year old with military leanings: 'A tent bed with black and red damask hangings, 3 arm chairs, a little folding table, blew window hangings, a looking glass, eleven pictures'. His eldest sister, who half a century later was to inherit Tarbat estates and the rebuilt house, had her own room, with a standing bed 'hung with blew', and '4 pairs of blew and white plaids' on the bed. The three next daughters (who eventually went to America after the family lost the property), had a simple room with 'two folding beds with yeallow turky hinging', and a cabinet and little tea table; the room also held 'eleven pictures of one kind or another', and a spinnet. Lord Cromartie had a masculine sort of study, called *My Lord's Closet*, containing 'an arm chair with a convenience in it' (who *did* empty all these conveniences?), 'a large book of maps' (but no other books recorded), 'a chimney glass, five old gunns ... three staves' (probably what a later fancy calls Lochaber axes, still used to decorative effect in old castles), '39 prints of one kind or another'. Outside, 'in the Lobie at my Lord's Closet door' were hung '4 prints, 35 pictures, 3 long pieces of landskips, a fine clock' (an old friend from 1695?) and 'two lead heads' earlier listed as cisterns. The 'anti-chamber' held the same furniture as in his father's day, but the dozen Russian leather chairs (which were earlier and perhaps more accurately described as Spanish leather) were all placed there. The 'Bigg dining room' had nothing in it, however, but 'one large chimney-glass'. Perhaps it is the same room as the Bigg Roome of the 1719 Inventar, which was crammed with dumped items then. Meddat had undoubtedly whisked some valuables and portraits out of sight before the official inventory was taken.

Lady Cromartie's own room had

'crimson velvet bed lined with green satin', lavishly equipped with bedding, including '$4\frac{1}{2}$ plaids cross-barred green, a green scattin quilt, a cabinet wt. a glass door and corner cupboard with a glass door, a large looking-glass, a mahogany corner table, a tea table ditto, and 6 chairs, 2 armchairs the same as the bed, a grate, a shovel and poking [fire irons], two little sconces, 4 pictures, two little stools [on which we hope the small girls sat to watch their mother dressing] a fire-screne on a mahogany stalk.

Very contemporary. There were two other dining rooms, so the emptiness of 'the Bigg dining room' is understandable. One held a large mahogany dining table, a card table and a marble table and a dozen chairs with leather bottoms, and '48 pictures of the Turkish Kings with the twelve apostles all in black.' In the Marble Dining Room there were ten gilt leather chairs; a mahogany tea table, orange stuff window curtains and 19 prints. It sounds a well-ordered and elegant household of the mid eighteenth century, with several items made of the new mahogany, taking the place of the old-fashioned walnut. But what *were* the subjects of all those pictures and prints?

Over the next few years there are a few short inventories of things sent to London, to the Earl and Countess in their imprisonment in the Tower and later in London. The most chilling item in an early list of domestic requirements is 'The hammer cloth and mourning of a hearse, in three pieces'. George's head was at risk from the axe of the Headman, and Lady Isabella was determined to put up a brave show. In 1750, when the threat of execution had been ameliorated to banishment, Mistress Meddat was allowed to send a few more things of a practical sort, 'blankets, the large floar carpet, the quilted cover and twillet'; some silver, such as 'a tea-kettle, spoons, sugar, caster and candlesticks'. The Earl kept writing for more furniture to be sent, though it is not clear if he got it all. In 1751 a larger consignment was permitted to be despatched, by the Commissioners for The Forfeited Estates, which included (probably) one of the Japanned lacquer chests, described as 'an Indian chist, but not its frame'—India and Japan were all parts of the mysterious East, served by East Indiamen, and so the interchange of descriptions need not bother us; they were confusions common up to the middle of the eighteenth century.

The grip of the Commissioners tightened. The estates were formally annexed to the Crown, and a semi-literate but perceptive clerk made yet another Inventar on 6 December 1750. In the four years since Munro of Teanninich had made his first Inventar it is clear that more than the handful of goods sent to London had been spirited away. Probably Meddat in collusion with John Gorrie, his opposite number on the Invergordon estates of Lady Bel's father, had been responsible. There is no written evidence, only a strong family tradition that 'our people and Gordon's' saved the family portraits, the papers, books and some of the best furniture. Certainly the portraits and papers survive as mute witnesses to this day.

The next list of 1754 shows very depleted rooms; for example in Lord MacLeod's room there is no sign of the smart tent-bed with black and red hangings, all that is left is 'a small folding wanscot table and eleven black and white prints'. Lady Bel's room has two folding beds—surely moved in by the servants to fill in the obvious gap, and an unlikely 'square painted black and yellow table', valued at 3 shillings and sixpence, and 'a chest of fineired drawers with a cabinet on the head'—was it the marquetry veneered tall-boy going back to Queen Anne's day? It was valued at five guineas. Another 'walnut tree cabinet' was in the garret with the servants' beds and valued at £2 2s. 6d., a measure of changing fashion.

Finally in this sequence there is the melancholy list of purchases made at The Roup of New Tarbat House. Roup is still the Scots word for an Auction sale. Things went for a song, and it looks as if more of the better pieces had disappeared. Most of the purchasers, whose names are all recorded, were supporters of the Cromartie family interest, such as Mistress Gorrie and several of the name of Mackenzie. Michael Stronach in Tarbat, surely a descendent of the master mason Stronach, bought three chairs and the cabinet from Lady Bel's room, and 'a small press in the garret'— it is tempting to think he had a good eye for a bargain and got the walnut, and he only paid a total of £2 15s. 6d. for the lot. Some humbler friends got bargains too: many bought plaids or blankets. Hugh Wilson, Tailor in Portlich, paid 3s. 6d. for '3 broken pans' and D Mcnaughton in Meddat gave a shilling for the kitchen table. Gregor Grant in Pollo bought 'a stool for 5 pence'. A few pieces evidently not in the sale were sold privately a few weeks later, such as a number of items to Mr Gordon, Younger of Ardoch, who took some of the pictures, and at last we get a chance to hear some of the subjects. He bought:

> A picture of clocks and rabbits in gilt frame
> A cook's shop in a gilt frame
> A picture of a Fool with a cabbage stock in black frame
> 2 pictures in fine gilt frames, one of them the History of Our Saviour in the
>   Temple, the oy. not known.
> A picture in a gilt frame above my Lady's closet door
> King Hendries picture, the Eight, in a gilt frame
> A small picture
> A tent bed with silk hangings
> A chamber box with casters.

The total sum of these items, most of which were probably late seventeenth century Dutch paintings, was £16 18s. 0d.

When the new house of Tarbat was built at the very end of the century, an inventory of some of the things saved by the Gordons of Invergordon was made, including the family portraits and 'a large mahogany bookcase with a press under, containing Cromartie's library of books'. These had not been mentioned in the inventory since the death of the first earl.

The furnishing of the Tarbat House of 1796 has no part in this tale of the old house.

The Gardens of Tarbat

The best evidence we have for the elaborate lay-out of the gardens of New Tarbat is contained in the map of the Barony made by Peter May for the Forfeited Estate Commissioners in 1754. The plans and plantings made by the first Earl, ignored by the second and revived by the third were, when the map was made, mature and at their prime. It is sad that we know so little about the gardeners themselves, for the head gardener at the start of such an ambitious scheme would have been a man of skill, a good plantsman. We have the names of several gardeners, one in particular was there for years, from the 1680s. William Frogg (surely an Englishman) was also entrusted with affairs beyond the garden gates; he supervised at least one big despatch of bere barley, he lent money to the cook in Edinburgh, and quite often signs as a witness to documents. Once he crops up in the Earl's service in London when Lady Wemyss was ill, and there is a John Frogg glancingly referred to, and another reference to a William Frogg, *physician* in Apidauld, which was just beyond the big house—had Frogg a side-line in herbal remedies? He died in 1718 according to Norman MacLeod the Factor, who wrote to Earl John that 'your gairdner old William Frogg was buried last week so shall your lordship look out for another servant in his statione, and if it is your desyre to live here this sumer it is proper you send seed to be sown accordingly.' As he wrote on 30 July it is as well that he covered himself by adding 'Your lordship is the best judge of quality and quantity. The children, blissed be, are well.' It is to be feared that by this date the gardens were already run-down and neglected. In November of the same year Lord Reay, a family friend and protestant soldier of note had called at the House, and was moved to write afterwards:

> Since your lordship dont design, as you told me, to finish your gardens and that the statues and gates are useless to you and will spoil, if you incline to dispose of them, I'll find you a merchant.

19   Map made by Peter May, Surveyor to the Annexed Estates, in 1755, showing New Tarbat House and surrounding farms.

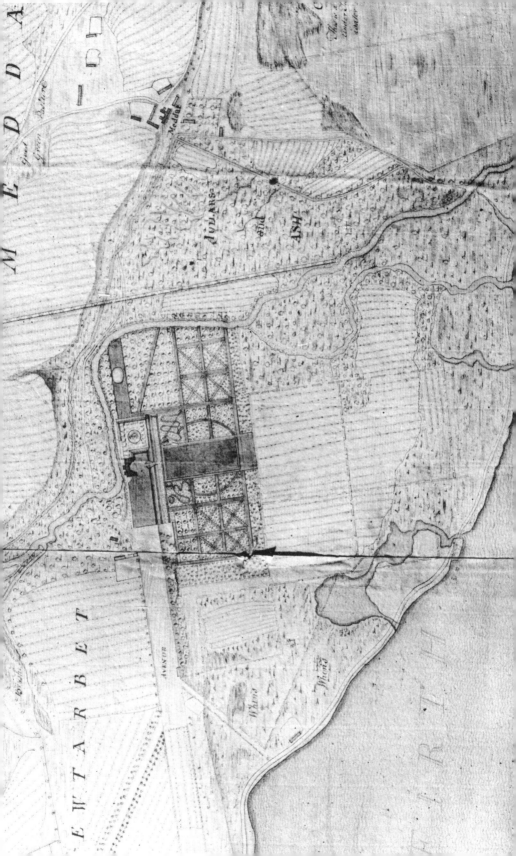

John did not design, nor did he put himself to the trouble of writing back to Lord Reay to arrange the disposal of the statues. Lord Reay wrote again about them the following year, but they remained in place until the Forfeiture of 1746.

The lay-out as revealed on the map is stamped with the hand of George the first Earl, and was naturally in the Baroque formal manner of the seventeenth century of his youth, rather than a realisation of the rococco 'capabilities' of the eighteenth century. Below the stone terrace, on which we can suppose the first Earl visualised walking with his friends and his dogs on calm summer evenings (in a manner harking back to his early visit to Italy in 1656), was a complicated knot-garden outlined in bold curves by little hedges, probably of box. It must have resembled Pitmedden, now the best surviving Scottish example. The original garden at Pitmedden was exactly contemporary with New Tarbat. It was built in 1674 by Sir Alexander Seton, whose career was rather similar to Tarbat's: he also was a cavalier, and had travelled extensively on the continent during the Commonwealth and had returned to prosperity on his Aberdeenshire estates. He was a friend and distant kinsman of Tarbat's, as they both were of Sir William Bruce, who finished his Royal commission to renovate the house and gardens of Holyroodhouse in Edinburgh in 1671. It is believed that a similar formal knot garden was designed there, and in other Edinburgh sites at this period. Bruce's own House of Kinross was not completed until 1690, and he then acknowledged his debt to Le Nôtre and the gardens of Vaux le Viscomte and Versailles, seen and admired during his Royalist exile in the 1650s. There is no evidence that either Seton or Tarbat saw these gardens, but both appear to have been influenced by Le Nôtre's concepts. Both built terraces above the parterres, to view the garden lay-out, and had pavillions, fountains, stairways and sundials. Robert Mylne was employed at Pitmedden as master mason; we have only a large bond paid to him by Tarbat for an unspecified reason as evidence that he worked for Tarbat, but if Mylne did work for him it would most likely have been at Royston. The garden at Pitmedden is today a learned reconstruction (using, however, modern plant material) of Seton's Great Garden of 1674. From the detailed evidence of Peter May's map of the garden at New Tarbat though, the parterres there were much more flowing than those at Pitmedden today, with overall arabesques rather than balanced formality. There is no surviving record of the plants used to arrive at these effects.

The sweep in front of the house was the setting for the great statue in lead of *Cain and Abel* and there were other lead figures, one of Neptune and others unknown. The first Earl had also designed to have a fountain, again a rather Italianate conceit from a country where artificial showers were more appreciated than in Ross-shire. He had ordered it, or at least talked of it, at the time he was dealing with the London sculptor Ibrach who was making the memorial to his second wife, in 1706, but it was delayed and re-ordered in a rush from Matthew Redhead in London. The agreement called for:

> A water ingan (engine) according to Sir John Mayor's pattern as good in all respects as that was when first made of brass and iron and led to force water thirty or forty feet high through a pipe two inches boore or more if required, and also three figures, one a man and two wimmen wone with a (moon?) and the other a swan standing by them and the man with the sunn at his feet al three five foot high and more and also twenty yeards of lead pipes 2 inches boord at two pence the pound, the three figures and Ingen coming to twenty-five pounds to be made in one month from this date 25 July 1711, London.

Though the maker must have been prompt and the Earl had paid him £25 sterling for the Engine and it is recorded as part of the cargo of goods from Royston to New Tarbat in 1712, it was never put up and the boxes lay about (noted in several inventories), disappearing about the time of the Forty-five when spare lead was much in demand.

Beyond the gravel sweep with Cain and Abel on their pedestal and the terrace and the arabesques of the formal parterre, the Tarbat gardens were set out in Baconian order, with curved nut-walks, fruit trees planted quincunx, others pleached or trained to the garden walls. Beyond was a 'Wilderness' and plantations of timber and lesser groves of aller (alder) and willow. It all faced south and was sheltered from the north and west. The kitchen garden is not distinct on the map but we can assume its existence. The plantation of willows was practical, pollarded for a multitude of uses as withies, or for basket-making or for the wickerwork divisions of cottages, whose interior walls were often of willow plastered with mud and lime-washed. Beyond the confines of the garden the first Earl planted many trees, some of them such as limes were exotics in Ross at that time. A formal park with great free-standing trees was essential, they advertised to every passer-by that a great mansion stood within: this display was necessary to the show of consequence which was a main object in the building of New Tarbat and its policies. Apart from a few minor offences heard in the Baron Baillie court of cutting trees and lifting turfs from the borders of the policies there is scarcely any mention of the trees until they were assessed for felling in 1760.

The tilling and general maintenance of so ambitious a garden must have been hard work. The records are scanty. The ten spades bought from the obliging general merchant, Hossack, in Inverness (along with two quires of paper and four four-gallon barrels) may have been for the garden. Oxen were purchased about the same time in the early eighteenth century, for the home-farm ploughing, in pairs of five; these could have been released for work during the lay-out of the policies, though they would hardly have been handy after the garden was planted. Curiously it is clear that the Highland breast-plough, the cas-chrom, was not in use at all in Easter Ross. Gorrie, the factor of Invergordon wrote in 1757 to his opposite number, Mackenzie of Meddat on behalf of his Principal, Hamilton Gordon of Newhall. Mr Gordon had asked Meddat to

> ... get two men from Coigeach to work at Newhall wt. what they call ye cassychrom for taking up whins, etc, in ground he means to plant in the wilderness way. He saw in his going south some sich men at Kilraich [Kilravoch, Nairn] which pleased him much and therefore he expects you'll provide him wt some hands of this kind as soon as possible, who will be paid for their work weekly.

This comment is another instance of the great barrier that the mountains of mid-Ross presented. In the eighteenth century men spoke of 'the Highlands' meaning Wester Ross, and the 'Lowlands' meaning Easter Ross.

There is not much evidence of soft-fruit growing, but Mr Hossack supplied many orders for sugar-loaves, and there was a large number of glass and pottery preserving jars in inventories in the pantry. The recipe books include a number of currant and raspberry conserves and jellies. When Cadboll was leasing Castle Leod he wrote one July to Meddat requesting him to send the gardener over to oversee the picking of fruit, 'As it is more reasonable that I should have it than the Dingwall skirmishers'.

When George came into possession of New Tarbat on his coming of age and marriage in 1725 (and becoming Earl on the death of his father in 1731), there was a great revival of interest in the house and gardens. His father and step-mother removed to Castle Leod and young Lord Tarbat and his Lady Bel proceeded to give the house a great cleaning and refurbishing. The gardens were also put back in order, and the banks cleared of encroaching whin bushes. Somewhere among the litter of packing cases still in the house, relics of his grandfather's day, Tarbat came across 'the iron gate and the head of the gate' which had been shipped up from Royston in 1712. He immediately gave orders to the Stronach of the day to build up two gateposts, with pedestals, cornices and terminal globes of stone, from a selected quarry in Morayshire, where Stronach was to go to choose it, for mounting the iron gateway. His instructions are detailed, a little fussy. He also gave orders for the rebuilding of the gable end of the house 'which was old work' and for harling the exterior of the house. No sign of the gateway remains.

Captain Forbes of New, the Forfeited Estates' Factor to the Annexed Estates of Lovat and Cromartie was, after his appointment in 1751, often concerned with the policies of New Tarbat. 'Policies' is the good Scots term for the grounds of a mansion house. At the first dilatory settlement of the estate accounts in October 1749 one of the claims allowed was to 'John Hall, Gardener at New Tarbat, the sum of £32 10s. 5¼d. as Wages to him and gardener servants.' He was not actually paid the money until 1753: it seems unlikely that he would have kept on the extra men, or kept up the garden in top condition for eight years after his master had disappeared into the Tower of London, though his best hope of payment must have been to continue in his post.

The flowering plants which must have been grown for three generations at New Tarbat have left no trace, either on the ground, or in the correspondence, though we know bulbs and slips of exotic plants were grown at Royston, and it is tempting to assume they were also grown in Rossshire. We do have evidence of the bigger trees in a Factor's letter of 5 February 1760, written in response to a Petition from an iron-founder, Robert Bull, who wished to use the neglected 'barren timber on the Mains of New Tarbat' for smelting. This was before widespread knowledge of Abraham Derby's revolutionary discovery of coke-smelting took the constant pressure off ironmasters to find new sources of charcoal for smelting. The Board endorsed Bull's petition and passed it to the Factor to report: Forbes replied:

> I went myself and inspected the Barren Timber fit for sale at New Tarbat, and employed proper persons to number and value all that could be sold without disfiguring the Policy of the place and now I send you enclosed the report of the wood men. ... They suppose that the value of such trees as can be sold may account for £141.9. sterling after deducting £15 sterling for rooting out the young trees in the garden, but I hardly think they will scarcely yield so much ... I beg leave also to acquaint the Hon. Board that some time ago some wicked ffellowes have cutt off a part of the lead of one of the statues at New Tarbat, in the night time, and have disfigured one of them very much. It is a statue of Cain and Abel who stood before the entry of the house and it is a pity that such insolence should pass unpunished. I caused make a search soon after the thing was done, and having found some lead with two or three ffellowes in the neighbourhood which appears the very same taken from the statue I thought it proper to cause take a Precondition (law proceedings) before the Sheriff ... it is the more necessary to insist because some time ago there was an Arm cutt from another of the statues of which no discovery was made.

The account enclosed for the *Standing Timber at New Tarbat Fitt for Cutting* extends for three pages, summarised on the fourth page as 'A Particular Accn of the solid contents of the different kinds of trees and deduction thereof for Bark, etc, Measured and numbered by Alex Sangster at

Balnagowan and Daneil Sanderson, Joiner in Cromarty and ... priced by them as follows':

Number of Trees	Solid Feet	Deduct for Bark	Solid Clean Timber (feet)	Price per foot	TOTAL (sterling)
90 Ashes	$2320\frac{3}{4}$	464	1856	6d.	£46. 8. 0
22 Elms	$192\frac{1}{2}$	$38\frac{1}{2}$	154	8d.	5. 2. 8
37 Plains	$295\frac{1}{2}$	59	236	5d.	4. 18. 4
23 Limes	$259\frac{3}{4}$	52	$207\frac{1}{2}$	5d.	—
45 Abells	551	110	441	—	—
400 Allers @ 1/- each					20 0 0
400 Allers 6d. each					10 0 0
400 Allers 3d. each					5 0 0

Sangster and Sanderson go on to justify their pricing, which included 'a number of young forest trees in and about the garden of New Tarbat which may be cut down without hurting the Policy' as 'supposedly' worth £50 sterling, and make a total offer of £141. 09s. 10d. sterling. They point out that they have measured but not priced the Limes and Abells (white poplar) as 'such wood is not commonly sold or used in this country therefore we do not pretend to be proper judges of its value'. The clear picture is conveyed of a derelict garden and park, over-run with the native scrub of alder and whin and self-seeded sycamores ('Plains', in the list). It was the end of the first garden so carefully laid out by the first Earl, and tended by William Frogg.

The house and policies of New Tarbat were let in 1766 to Dr Mackenzie, a tenant who was put in possession of a part of the Mains of Tarbat and of the East Wing of the house ... 'he has enclosed and is improving his small farm to good purpose'. Was he cultivating the walled garden?

Merchants, Ministers and Mariners

The first Earl was a gregarious man, with friends in many quarters. His political allies, the peer-group of the Scots nobility, is quite well documented. Less well known are his friends in many walks of life, out of which it is easy to select a few to represent three categories: the merchants, the ministers, and the sea-captains. The merchants cover a wide range from the minor suppliers of household needs in Inverness or Tain to the high and mighty merchants of Edinburgh, some destined soon to join the nobility like William Binning.

In the Lairds' Loft of Tarbat parish church there are two small memorial tablets. One is to Sir John Mackenzie of Tarbat, who worshipped there until his death in 1654, the other to the grain-merchant John Cuthbert. Cuthbert migrated from Tarbat to the centre of Inverness about the time of Sir John's death, and was the progenitor of a long line of solid Inverness burgesses who lived at Castle Hill, just south of the burgh. He and Tarbat did a lot of business together; lending money, exchanging Bonds, particularly at the time that Sir George was pursuing the Urquhart family and needed cash quite often. Cuthbert also underwrote part of the swingeing fine imposed by Government on the head of the Mackenzie clan, the Earl of Seaforth, after the failure of the Glencairn Rising in 1654. Seaforth had passed on the fine to many members of his clan, cautioners for his bond. The Cuthberts eventually felt they had had enough prevarication and required repayment and instituted a claim in Court. Tarbat however, wrote, an exceedingly civil letter, on 8 December 1680, to John Cuthbert, Town Clerk of Inverness:

> Sir I am disappointed of some money I expected, else I had provyded and sent £500, which since I promised I will perform as soon as it be possible ... I hope we shall be at a period in our action (for since both our actions are just) in seeing payment, if ye winne ye shall weare it without the least grudgein. Sir, your affectionate Friend, Tarbat.

One could hardly wish for a more civil letter from a man you had in the courts for non-payment of a large debt, dating back a quarter of a century. Tarbat, perennially in debt, never lapsed into a formula in advising any delay in repayment. Each letter is pristine and carefully thought-out for the circumstances. Some of the humbler creditors were the least softened by this treatment. We do not have the letter written to William Darson, who was roofing part of Castle Leod in 1690; judging from his reply it did not impress him: Darson began by complaining that the chamberlain had not honoured the agreement made between him and Lord Tarbat for the sarking. ('Sarking' is the undercladding of planks beneath a slated roof.)

> Your lordship be pleased to offer me more work in this place or else gibe me wadgery for byegone work, and yet I may look for your service, hoping this will not be neglected to the disadvantage of Wm. Dason. P.S. I want a half-firlot of meal every week, which I should gett.

Another local merchant who moved from Tarbat parish to Inverness was Thomas Hossack who is never beguiled into replying to quite chatty letters from his noble customers. He enjoyed much business with The Master. His business seems to have been a general grocery and Vintners. For example on 20 December 1689, John, The Master of Tarbat, wrote a conversational letter:

> I heard that there is some Rhenish wine com be Broune (a sea captain) but that the Governor and Captaine Forbes has taken it all, Colline (Seaforth) told me he thought you would prevail wt. the captain for a quart of it likewise I entret you, if you could get but a bottle of it, try ...

The letter is dated the Chanonrie, i.e. Fortrose, where at that date The Master was under house-arrest for his part in an abortive plot to join up with the Marquis of Dundee; he was directly imprisoned in the charge of General MacKay, Governor of the Citadel of Inverness, and Captain Forbes. Hossack in his usual laconic way merely endorsed the letter. 'Sent 4 chop. Rhen. wine at £3. 0. 0.'.

Earlier in the same year, before the hint of treasonable rising was abroad, The Master had written to Hossack a rambling letter about a half anker of Brandy, 'be pleased to give the bearer' who was provided with an empty small barrel.

> I desire you likewise to give the bearer 4 pounds of courants, 4 pounds of raisings, 4 pounds of rice, an pound of pepper, half an ounce of rock Indegor. I instruct you'll see them carefully put up that they be not mixt ...

Hossack, not mellowed even by the signature of his 'assured friend and servant John Tarbat' merely endorsed the letter:

Sent:
4 lb Raisin
1 lb peper
$\frac{1}{2}$ oz sable indigo
2 oz nuttmegges.

There are several other bills which include indigo, and one for Azure Blue: were the ladies of Tarbat House dying their own tartans? Indigo, especially the dark 'black' or navy kind is the one dye unobtainable from any local source. There is no other evidence. Hossack on other occasions supplied spices, ginger, sugar loaves, quires of paper and, once, six packs of playing cards. Other local merchants tended not to waste words. John Barne in Malabost in the Lewes received a brief communication from Lord Tarbat: 'Send me 100 of the best and fattest ling that run ... and by this order my chamberlain in Coigach to pay you one price for which this shall be warrant'. The letter is dated 17 November 1688 from Royston, and is receipted in Dingwall in February 1690. There was no resident chamberlain in Coigach which must have made recovery of this sum quite difficult. The amount is not stated.

There was a small group of merchants whom Lord Tarbat was actively trying to encourage in infant industries in Scotland, by investment and by promotion among his friends and even by private members' bills in the Scottish Parliament. One of the most promising of these ventures was The Leith Glass Works, started in 1689, with a printed *Proclamation in Favour of Glassworks*. The manufacturer was Alex Ainsley, who had been sent to Holland and to Deptford to learn the craft. Tarbat was the principal shareholder and promoter, although there is evidence of a copartnery in 1689. By 1690 green glass bottles were being produced for sale, and a list of customers all over the east of Scotland was built up, running as far afield as an apothecary in Kirkwall, Orkney. The customers were either the gentry—those who could afford to buy wine by the hogshead and decant it—or physicians and apothecaries who had medicines to give out. Tarbat had friends and acquaintances in quantity in both categories. Unfortunately after a few years the Glass Works came to grief through the import and dumping of English bottles and, as A Ainslie protested, the illegal harassment of having many troops billeted on him in the Works. Not much better luck attended other investments: neither paper works, Alex Simpson's shot-casting works; nor the Linen Manufactory of Nicholas Derain, who wrote in friendly terms to Lord Tarbat (a major shareholder) in March 1694 that he had 'taken Deray Mills House within a mile of Edinburgh ... and I have had several meetings with the gentlemen-subscribers to the Scotts Linen Manufactory.'

There is a copy of a will made by one of these gentlemen-subscribers, a Doctor Alex Brown who was going to the East Indies in the ship *Bedford* in 1698, and after bequeathing a gold mourning ring and £20 Sterling to each of a list of friends which started with Lord Tarbat, Dr Pitcairne, Dr Gregorie and Dr Andrew Welsh of St Maries, Spain, he left the remainder to the town of Kirkcaldy for the setting up of a fishery and a linen manufactory. His trustees were to 'Advance the interest of that which may prove beneficial to the nations in general and the product of either or both, I mean the fisheries and linnen manufacture.' This Dr Brown was a relative of the Browns and also apparently of the Bruces, into which families two of Tarbat's daughters married.

Tarbat also showed a great interest in establishing fisheries off the Scottish coasts, particularly those based in Ullapool. He was a century in advance of his time, and his efforts were hopelessly unsuccessful. Neither transport for the finished barrels of herring nor any well developed demand for the product could be found, let alone enough capital in the 1690s. Tarbat's partner in the fishing endeavour was Sir William Binning of Bavelaw, an 'upwardly mobile' burgess friend in Edinburgh with property in the Pentland Hills. Tarbat occasionally bought hay and forage for his horse-feed at Royston from him and they corresponded amicably on gardens and farming, including the use of turnips as winter feed. Tarbat meditated on the state of Scotland and of its economies in particular—the word 'economy' had not yet become common coinage. Tarbat was a mercantilist of the central school, and his writings in that mode are persuasive and thoughtful. He considered that the weakness of the Scottish nation derived from reliance on imported secondary goods, such as linen, and her export of primary unprocessed ones; he was concerned about the hides that went abroad, not tanned nor made into shoes, he said.

Scarcity of coin, and the competition of the English markets, above all the denial (by the English) of any Scots access to foreign shipping and colonial markets in Asia and America worried him most. He was one of the most ardent advocates of the *Company of Adventurers Trading to Asia and Africa*, the promoters of what is now known as the Darien Scheme. His brother Roderick Mackenzie, Lord Prestonhall, was the secretary to the *Adventurers*, and Tarbat and each of his family invested up to the maximum permitted in the Venture. It was a total disaster, for Scotland and for the Mackenzie family. Again Tarbat's thinking seems to have been ahead of his contemporaries, but unviable in the event. The Cromartie correspondence contains a number of letters on this topic, and also on the collection for the Hearth Tax and Poll taxes, two unpopular measures of 'King William's ill years'. Tarbat held the farm of tax for the shires of Ross & Cromarty, in partnership with two other magnates—there was much bickering, and the mechanics of collection came under criticism. The collector, Bayne, gave in his final total for the parishes of east and central Ross-shire, saying that the collector 'Long John MacRae' appointed for the six parishes of the west had not returned anything at all, and seemed unlikely to do so. Another whole category of merchant partners and business associates were connected with the lucrative fishing of the waters of Conon, including Inverness magnates such as Duff, Robertson and Mackintosh, and the original leasor Sir Thomas Calder.

Ministers and Clergy

The contacts with the Ministers of the Church of Scotland were varied. Tarbat had inherited the rights to the Bishops' Teinds (tithes) which included the right of presentation of a minister to fourteen parishes in Ross. He lived through the divisive Civil Wars of his youth with the extremists of presbyterianism and episcopacy fighting it out in battle; the placid years of the Restoration exactly suited his temperament, which was devout, authoritarian, episcopalian and inclined to reject the fierce inherent democracy of the presbyterians. He genuinely abhored the presbyterian rejection of the Liturgy, which was then so extreme that a commited presbyterian of the 1690s considered the use of the Lord's Prayer to be liturgical and popish, and rejected it accordingly. As patron of these parishes in Ross, however, he had to provide ministers who were acceptable to most of the parishioners.

Bishop Rose of Edinburgh, together with Lord Tarbat as a leading Scottish layman, was bidden to wait on the new King William in Kensington, after King James VII and II had 'gone overseas', in the rebellion the English called 'glorious'. 'I trust', said the new King, 'That the Bishops of Scotland will be as kind to Me as their brothers in England have shewn themselves'. Quaking the bishop answered stoutly that the Church of Scotland would serve the new King 'As far as conscience and the law would permit'. The old episcopal church of Scotland held to the Stuarts who had supported it, and even more deeply, they believed that an oath of allegience, once given, should be kept. It was not until James had sent from France in 1690 to absolve some of the Highland chiefs and clergy of their oaths that they could in honour swear to keep King William's peace. King William's distrust of and boredom with Scottish affairs deepened, and he acquiesced with his Secretary's wishes and disestablished the Episcopal Church, creating in its place The Presbyterian Church of Scotland, 'By Law Established'.

This threw out of the manses of Scotland a number of divines who, along with Bishop Rose, felt they could agree with a law-keeping government, such as King William offered—a protestant government, which was more than James had guaranteed in his last years—but they could *not* overlook the oath they had sworn on induction; nor could they forget the Biblical injunction about the Right of the First-Born Son. Presbyterians also had real qualms about this undeniable piece of Scripture: if the King disregarded the right of the first-born, where would any of them be in terms of their own families' inheritance? In a strictly patriarchal society it was a key question, a cornerstone question for eldest sons and heads of households.

A number of the displaced clergy, from the Bishops downwards, wrote to Lord Tarbat for help in applications for pensions from the Crown. As it was Archbishop Sharp who had helped Tarbat back into state service in the 1670s he had a debt to repay. He was known to be in favour with King William, and to be a staunch follower of episcopy himself. It seems, however, that these petitioners may have been disappointed. Tarbat was himself manoeuvering on slippery ground; his son was under house arrest for Jacobite plotting, and his own pension had not been paid regularly. There is little trace of replies to the letters of the distressed clergy, though this is not to say that he did nothing for them. There is a draft of a paper to be presented to the Queen's Majesty in 1704, on the payment of Bishops' Rents, the up-taking of such rents by the Laity, and needs of indigent episcopalian clergy. It is endorsed by the newly made Earl: 'Scroll of a proposal for ye Bishops' Rents in Scotland'. Since his own branch of the Mackenzies together with others of that ilk were the chief beneficiaries of the Teinds of the Bishops of Ross—and had been since 1560 or so—it was unlikely that he would have been enthusiastic for a different distribution. Ambivalence was a leading characteristic of this wily old statesman. Letters survive from all sorts of clergy: from the grand-daughter of the late Bishop Spottiswood of Glasgow; from a young minister of Kirkwall who had been 'Outed and had nothing beyond £16. Scots to live on for two years bypast'; and from the old bishop of Aberdeen is found a Memorial to Lord Tarbat: 'having suffered in common with his brethren by the act abolishing their government in the year 1689 he did begin to retire to a country living hoping under the shadow of the Government to live in peace and quiet.' This had not been possible, and he now petitioned Lord Tarbat, saying he was 'old and infirm and hath a numberous family ... he relies only on Lord Tarbat for his generous disposition to this afflicted church.'

Mackenzie of Inchculter wrote to the Earl on 21 September 1711 a letter so illustrative of the problems and the attitudes of the staunch episcopalian that it is worth quoting nearly in full,

> Your Lordship being Patron of the Church of Kilmuir Wester I give you the trouble of knowing the method taken yesterday for planting one Mr Grant, a presbyterian Minister there, by the Sheriff Kilravock and the pres-

bytrie. The right of calling to that parish being *jure devolute* fallen into the presbyterie's hands there was an edict 1st Lord's day placarded on the church door desiring all the heritors and parishioners to attend the presbyterie at Rosemarkie the 19th. They being there, all except (—) of Muirtton the only presbyterian in the parish, they did object: *primo*: that Mr Grant could not be imposed upon them, it being against the inclinationes of the whole parish (except one) they being Episcopall and that the inclinations of the people being the only basis of presbytery and the reason of the law, *ergo* it was illegal, 2dly that they could not comply with Mr Grant in his method of worship because he never did use the Lord's Prayer and in these things the Heritors and whole parishioners did protest against Mr Grant and desired their protestation might be insert in the Presbytry's books, which was allowed.

Yet the next day the Sheriff proceeded with 24 men all armed wt. gunns, swords, pistolls and targetts, wt. a piper, came over Ardinfuir and went along with the presbytery and broke open the church door where Mr Grant was ordained and institute after their singular method ... but what I reflect on, is that when sheriffs soe begett presbyterians, we are all destitute, for I'm sure its against the rules of Christendom to settle a minister in a parish where none will have him, for the greed of gaining 20 or thrittie pound of stipend ... so much for the Kirk.

An earlier attempt to 'intrude' a minister to Urray in 1707, made by the presbyterian faction, was rejected with violence by the parishioners who boarded up the church to keep him out, and enlisted some of the tinkers camping near by to indulge in a 'Rabbling'. A worse rabbling had taken place in Dingwall in 1704, on the death of the loved old minister Jo MacCrae. By 1689, it should be remembered, the episcopalian faction had lost legal tenure to the presbyterian who were now the Church by Law Established, legally the top, the only recognised form. However, episcopalian parishes retained ministers of that persuasion if they could; support for the middle, episcopalian way of worship lingered a long time in Ross-shire. (The earlier example quoted, from Kilmuir, took place 20 years after the law was passed). A handful of Roman Catholics survived furtively, taking comfort from young Lord Seaforth, sent away by his young mother to France, who was being brought up a catholic. Fourteen of the leading Mackenzie lairds of the north, however, wrote to Tarbat, as next in succession, imploring him to use his influence to bring young Seaforth back to be educated a Protestant in Scotland. Catholics were extremely unpopular. The Mackenzies offered to pay for the young Chief's return. Lovat too was a covert catholic and, much to the sorrow of his father, John Master of Tarbat, became a secret convert too, offering a 'safe house' to passing priests, indeed the hospitality of the priest's hole in the thickness of the walls in Castle Leod. His father wrote a long temperate letter to his son begging him not to take this step (political dynamite as well as a danger to his eternal soul), and not to desert the teachings of the church in which he had been brought up.

There was a distinct whiff of the dangers of Rome in the air. For example there was the will of Donald Maclennan, latterly Minister of Fearn in Ross. He left at his death in March 1689:

> 8 young beasts [cattle]
> 2 garrons [Highland ponies]
> 6 silver spoon and twa silver dishes, estimate all at £40
> Ane little aquavitis; estimate £2 [probably a small still]
> ane little mortar: £3
> All the defunct's librar and books: estimate to £40

This will led to complications. First Donald's brother died. He was also a churchman, Rev Fergie MacLennan, Archdeacon of the Isles, and the brothers appear to have left their estates to the same nephews, Rev Fergie adding a sum to a 'neighbour-germane in Ochterneed', and promising 4,000 merks conditionally to another member of the family: 'Kenneth MacLennan ... who went abroad to trabbel about thirty-four years agon, should (he) happen to return to this Kingdom without entering into the orders of the Romish Church'. A formal and complex document, amplifying the will in respect to Rev Fergie's intentions towards his nephew, was drawn up and signed at Royston House, in the presence of Lord Tarbat, and witnessed by the Minister of Foddertie, John Mackenzie, who had been appointed Archdeacon, and by Colin Mackenzie, a lawyer, before being registered 'for mair security' in the Books of Council. The next heard of the recusant priest Kenneth was indirectly in a claim entered by two other Edinburgh lawyers on behalf of 'one of the nephews'— unnamed. They alleged that the late Minister of Fearn had been a grain and cattle dealer and had large sums of money outstanding to their client. They adduced the evidence, over two closely written pages. They claimed 4,000 merks on behalf of their client, a sum suspicious because of its identity with the roving Kenneth's bequest. No more is heard of these papers.

More usual in the correspondence are letters about the mundane business of collecting the stipend of the ministers: this was in theory the business of the Patron, Lord Tarbat, but he, like many other crafty landlords had handed the obligation on to his tenants as a part of their rent though it enhanced their social standing. The ministers had to return a receipt to Tarbat, and thus John Mackenzie of Foddertie wrote, in 1667 that he had had '26 bolls of barley, not the full amount, and likewise had received from a tenant fourtie merks Scots ... and also I got a Band [bond: note of hand] from Angus Macdonald for the money rent of Ulladale and Kinitas.'

This was before the days when Rev John Mackenzie was 'swoln into the dignity of an Archdeacon', in the words Rev Thomas Kennedy used about him nearly two hundred years later. Kennedy, a founder of the Free Church in Ross, wrote scathingly about all the ministers of the Restoration period.

Old Cromartie, the first Earl must have had a qualm of conscience about his treatment of the ministers in his patronage, for about two months before his death in 1714 he drew up a document commending—commanding—the repair of all churches and manses, and the payment of all outstanding dues in this connection: the cost, however, was not to be borne by the Cromartie estates but by the Heritors and tenants in each parish. He had paid for repairs to the Clement Aisle in Dingwall where his father was buried, for the roof at Tarbat Kirk and for the roof and gable-end at Wester Kilmuir. The manse at Kiltearn, however, was left particularly ruinous, almost uninhabitable, but then that parish was stubbornly presbyterian, so apparently came low on any list for the Patron's bounty.

Shortly before his death the first Earl was sent a draft copy of the 1712 Patronage Act (Scotland), the act which led to more than a century of internal strife between Patrons, Heritors and the members of the parish churches and finally was a root cause of the Disruption of 1843. He scrawled across it: 'This matter is merely civil *et eodum modo resolvitur quo compositum*'. He also wrote many prayers and religious reflections. In one he remarked that:

> The unconsidering Atheist is no rarity: for all who live as if there were not ane omniscent and omnipotent Judge to whom they must shortly answer ... [are such].

The second Earl kept up his father's interests in the affairs of the Kirk, complicating life very much for the other Heritors of the parishes. For example David Ross of Inverchassely petitioned about the Teinds he had to pay the Minister of Logie Easter—miles from where he lived—'there being some jostle betwixt the Patron (Earl John) and Heritors ... in this our Petitioner is aggrieved beyond any other Heritor in the Parish'. This, though dated 28 July 1719, takes the grievance back to an obscure debate about the obligation of 9 bolls due from Drumgillie, which George, the first Earl, had sold (together with its obligation) in 1673, nearly fifty years before. In the next year, 1720, the schoolmaster of Culcairn named John Urquhart petitioned for the previous year's payment of his salary for the school in the parish of Kilmuir. Nothing had been paid: 'this was occasioned by your Lordship going south and not returning till I was obliged by want of encouragement to demitt my charge and leave the place

...'. The 'singular kindness' of the back payment of his salary (amounting to only 6 bolls of bere) for the whole year was petitioned.

Patronage, the 'matter merely civil', was a carefully cherished right, for the appointment of a parish minister was a great measure of social control. The Cromartie family fully appreciated this. In 1708 the old Earl buttressed his rights by putting in a Claim of Rights, supported by seventeen documents in evidence of his patronage of fourteen parishes.

In the course of Mackenzie of Meddat's careful handing over to the Commissioners for the Forfeited and Annexed estate Meddat made a list of the fourteen parishes. It was clear that by then many more had adopted the extreme presbyterian stand of Alness and Kiltearn and were not susceptible to any but a minister of extreme presbyterian views. Rev McKilligen of Alness had, after all, been imprisoned on the Bass Rock for some time for his faith. There were martyrs of all persuasions. The triumphant presbyterians, later moving into the disestablished ranks of the Free Church, have emphasised the past sufferings of their brethern. The efforts of, say, the women of Dingwall to stand up to '60 armed men, presbyterians', trying to intrude a successor to Rev J McCrae of episcopal persuasion have been forgotten, although the women were beaten 'to the effusion of blood'. Count Macleod, on his return in 1784 tried to re-establish his family's firm system of patronage, and his sister Lady Elibank took her claim to court, and lost.

Mariners

There are more than forty Contracts which survive, of which the majority are Charter Parties, made between Tarbat and a number of skippers in the coastal trade, for the conveying of cargoes from and to the Cromarty Firth. They date between 1660 and 1738, although there are very few after 1710. They and many other documents all relate to the grain trade on which so much of the family's fortune was based. The pattern was a regular one. At the feast of Candlemas, 2 February, or thereabouts, the chamberlains of the estates took in the rent, in victual from Tarbat and Strathpeffer. In practice this was all in bere barley. The gap between the end of the harvest, and the late gathering of the rent is accounted for by the obligation the tenants had to supply the grain 'dight, raused and dried', in plain terms the grain had to be winnowed out of the ear by the use of hand-flails, and then dried in peat-fired kilns attached to the bigger barn-yards of the estates before being bagged and brought in and measured. This took up the whole winter, in laborious if warming work. The chamberlains had to measure the grain by the Great Boll of Tarbat, and to note any of the tenants who did not give in enough to write off their annual rent. Equally, the chamberlains were required to buy in, for cash, any surplus grain in their neighbourhoods, and to write to Lord Tarbat in Edinburgh, about the first week of March, acquainting him with the rough amount they expected to have to ship to Leith. Tarbat then negotiated a Contract to sell the bere to one of the great brewers of Leith, such as Cleghorne. The grain was to be delivered at the expense and risk of the vendor, so it behove Tarbat to deal with reliable skippers, and over the years a close connection was built up. However, there was nothing informal about the annual Charter Parties, drawn up in legal form in Royston, in which the Master of a named ship undertook to call at Cromarty, Dingwall, Portmahomack or several other little ports of the Firth, within a given time, a fortnight in May or June, and to lie at the port taking on board the cargo of so many bolls of bere, for ten weather-work days, and to return straight to the Port of Leith, at an agreed cost per boll. The names of the ships are standard, but delightful: the *Mary of Alloa, Rose of Aberdour, Witt of Kirkcaldy* and *Amitie of Inverness, Isobel of Findhorn* and others from all over the eastern seaboard of Scotland; the greatest number were from Leith. Once in port at Cromarty, Portmahomack or elsewhere there was a great rush to complete the loading within the stipulated 'weather work' days, that is not counting storm and stress, or Sabbath days. In only a few cases have we got detailed Bills of Lading: most of them are fairly curt. However, the Bill of Lading given by John Mackenzie, skipper of the *Marie of Alloway* (Alloa) in 1698 is fully detailed. Skipper Mackenzie shows up several times, notably in May 1692, taking on board part of the crop of 1691; he noted carefully after loading 263 bolls of bere and 22 bolls, 2 firlots oatmeal and 56 bolls oats ... 'Mynd ther is 8 bolls of the foresaif fiftie oats that do belong to a Cromartie merchant not to my Lord (Tarbat) ...'

The crop of 1698 was not quite so large: he gave receipt for loading:

    254 bolls good bere
     32 bolls oats
      2 bolls oatmeal in fourteen bags,
    And also a boll of meal and a barrill of Aile.

The writer added 'And so God send the good ship to Leith her desyred Port in Safety, written by Andrew Mackenzie lawfull son to the said skipper—April 1698'. On the back is a fuller breakdown, scribbled probably by Dan Mackenzie of Meddat, detailing the farms from which he shipped bere:

    Meddathill   4 Bolls
    Tullich   16

Kilmore	7	
Milntoune	8	
(———)	4	
Balasbragone	20	
Blackhill	4	
	——	
	63	
	——	
	4	
	——	
	67	

[This small amount from each must have been additional to the main rental: 'Bishops' teinds' perhaps.]

Andrew Mackenzie, the writer of his father's side of this document, was, according to his own account on another Bill of Lading, a Divinity student. Mackenzie, the Skipper of Alloa, had migrated south and entered the coal trade. (Shipping grain in a returning collier was apparently quite normal). Mackenzie brought several loads of coal to Dingwall, while other incoming cargoes were lime, for masonry, pig-iron and 'wanscotting', or shaped and cut timber for panelling both at Castle Leod (discharged at Dingwall), and Tarbat House (discharged at Delny). Rather late in the season of 1698, a most reliable skipper was selected for a special voyage. Skipper John Manners, of *Janet of Prestonpans* had already made one voyage early in April 1698 and picked up 353 bolls, with an additional 10 bolls from Cromarty for Leith. By the end of June he had picked up a more unusual cargo in Leith, a long list which included '20 lasts of oaken casks' (knock-down material for 240 casks) and great quantities of salt, a notoriously difficult cargo as it has to be kept dry. There were other necessities for the infant fishing station of Ullapool: ships' biscuit, lead shot, a gross of paper, a pound of sugar, 79 pound of Roll Tobacco, 16 gallons of Acquavity at 4 pence the pint. The value of this cargo, carefully computed, was £1661. 5s. 0d. Scots: it was landed safely at Stornoway and transhipped for Ullapool. Skipper Manners made a second voyage from Leith to Stornoway: the men of Wester Ross did not have dealings with the nearer port of Glasgow, at this date.

A Skipper called John Reid, first appears as Master and Sir Kenneth Mackenzie as part-owner, of 'the good bark called the *Hondred of Cromarty*'. This is the only local ship in these records and it may be a small one, as its freight was only 130 bolls, and 'four barells of salmon'. It was consigned directly to 'the Shores of Royston in the South Firth', and it was agreed to pay 'The caplagan average and other dues theirin ...' on 9 July 1707. *Caplagan*, spelt phonetically in a variety of ways, is a word not found in Scots dictionaries, though its meaning is clearly 'perquisite' or Master's due in all the shipping contexts in which it occurs. Another example is in the Charter between George Earl of Cromartie and Florence

Crawford, Skipper in Leith, who was to sail to St Colmshaven in Ross (Portmahomack) and there take a full freight of Bere to 'deliver to Leith or Fisherrow or where the Earl pleases at £8 per Chalder, and a boll of meal and a barrel of ale for Caplaigen'. Signed on 10 June 1706.

The year 1706 was a difficult one for the contracting parties, as a letter from MacLeod of Cadboll, acting for the landlord, the Earl, explained. There was a great deficit in the grain collected, not only had there been 'great and frequent rains' which damaged even the grain girnelled or in barns, but the wayward heir the Master of Tarbat had 'uplifted not less than 155 bolls out of a total deficit of 205, which he sold in a private proceeding'—not only running his father into the risk of defaulting with the parties in Edinburgh to whom he had already sold the corn, but allowing the crafty tenants to declare that they could not pay, as they alleged virtuously they had already paid their whole dues to The Master. No wonder Cadboll ended, 'It will be difficult'.

Skipper Reid (and later his son) seems to have been the most trusted of the Masters. Nearly forty years later, when the third Earl was released from the Tower of London and was trying to arrange the transport of his little daughter from Tarbat to London he wrote to Meddat: '*The Helen of Inverness* Capt Reid, Master, is expected here in 3 or 4 weeks I hope you will not miss that occasion as it is the best that can offer with respect to time and a careful Master, to send up the child Pegie and the goods contained in the list.' The son of Sir Kenneth Mackenzie of Cromartie married the daughter of Captain Reid of Cromarty, sea-captain; the connection between all these is now established and Captain Reid bought his handsome house still standing, called The Garden House, in Cromarty.

Neither Reid nor John Manners was entrusted with the most valuable cargo ever shipped by the Earl. This was the contents of Royston House, when he moved up to live permanently in the North. Part of the 'full lading' is given on pp. 83 and 84. The skipper entrusted with it was one John Morrison, but none of those ships' papers have survived, only the long inventory of his cargo, and a short note from the harassed secretary at Royston saying that he had had to charter another ship as Skipper Morrison had refused to take so much. As the decision to add the coach and harness for eight horses was only taken at the last moment, the skipper had justification. The rest of the cargo was consigned to a Skipper David Sibbald. The note on the reverse reads '… goods sent North in Monson's ship 1712 and David Sibbald's ship. The difference in spelling between Morrison and Monson should be a warning to genealogists not to rely on any scribbled evidence of this sort.

John Reid, Skipper in Leith, petitioned The Earl of Cromartie for a place as a Tidewaiter, a minor official in the Customs' service, putting forward his claim because one ship had been lost 'by Royston', probably

meaning on the coast there, which is an open anchorage, and that he had
had a ship burned in the year 1690 while taking provisions to the Royal
Army then in Ireland. Further, the Petitioner Reid (who seems to have
been accident-prone) 'being in the Downs the time of the late storm
received grat damage in his left hand which renders him incapable of
going about the employ whereto he was bred'. It is to be hoped that Reid's
request was passed on to the Lord High Treasurer of England, as he
petitioned. Cromartie had sent a whole year's grain crop to feed King
William's army in Ireland, and to establish his own loyalty, an investment
which paid well.

Military Matters

All through the period under review armies were on the march, and a very keen sense of the unrest of the day comes out of the papers. There were four main phases: firstly, the aftermath of the civil war and Glencairn's Rising (about which little direct evidence survives), secondly the troubled times after the ascension of William and Mary, during which the Highlands were in a state of ferment, and troops were billeted from 1688 until well into the 1720s on the suffering folk of Ross and Cromarty. The third military phase was of course during the Rising of 1745 and 1746, and the sequence comes full circle in the 1770s with the raising of two battalions of MacLeod's Highlanders to fight for King George, and to re-establish the heir in his estates. No consideration of the lives led in Ross during the hundred and fifty years under review would be complete without a few details of these military matters. The tradition of the Highland chief, able to call up his war-band was still alive, and a matter of some dread to the peaceable folk of Easter Ross who equated 'hyland-men' and 'clannit men' with war and menace. In fact the quartering of peaceable but demanding troops of the Crown probably did more damage.

The family papers do not reveal any thing about Sir John Mackenzie's participation in the Scottish army which went south with King Charles II and which was routed at the battle of Worcester on 3 September 1651, but it is known that Sir John and his eighteen year old son George were in the Royalist camp in that campaign. After the battle Protector Cromwell had forces garrisoning Scotland, who were successful in capturing nearly all the remaining members of the Scottish Committee of Estates at Alyth, shortly after news of Worcester. These acts virtually wiped out Scottish resistance, and Monck's army was the real ruler of the country. It was challenged two years later by Glencairn's Rising, which was specifically Highland in its origin, officered by clan chiefs and landowners in the north whose troops were their own war-like tenantry. Naturally the adherence of some clans to the Royalist cause made others with an hereditary antipathy to them stay neutral or side with Monck. At first the Model Army had little hold on the Highlands, and the Rising had successes. George Mackenzie, who inherited from his father in 1654, was an officer, and saw

much of the confused campaigning of the day. He welcomed General
Middleton to Tarbat when the exiled King Charles finally appointed him
as commander, and apparently sided with him and not in support of the
initial commander, Glencairn. By this time Seaforth had taken command
of the Clan Mackenzie hosts and the campaign was breaking down after
its initial successes. Col Lilburne, and then Col Monck himself, marched
his army through the wildest of Highland glens, even through the wastes
of Strathfarrar towards Eilean Donan, the Mackenzies' western fortress.
Cromwell had a Citadel built on the arm of the River Ness as it enters the
Firth at Inverness, and commanded a Government galley to be dragged
from that town to be launched on Loch Ness to patrol the shores. This
proved fatal to the Royalist Rising. Monck exacted heavy penalties.
Wariston, a contemporary commentator, said that in sending Monck to
command Cromwell 'would trye (Scotland) with rigor and ruyne'. Eilean
Donan castle was slighted, and the cornlands of the north were set on
fire and houses burned. Middleton's forces, and presumably Sir George
Mackenzie with them, managed to keep from a direct engagement though
the chase was hot and went over Ross, Inverness-shire and Perthshire.
Eventually an engagement was fought in the narrow pass of Dalnaspidal.
Most of the leading royalists managed to escape capture, and it is possible
that it was at this point that George Mackenzie and Sir Robert Moray
escaped to the west and eventually to the Hebrides though it may have
been later. Middleton though wounded escaped to Sutherland. Though
he returned to command, the Royalist Rising faded out in the face of
Monck's stringent patrolling and the internal divisions amongst the royalist
commanders. By 10 January 1655 Articles of Agreement were concluded
with Seaforth and several other Mackenzies: Glencairn and others had
already surrendered. Seaforth and the Mackenzies were, however, given
the right to keep their personal arms for their own defence and for the
keeping of law and order within their bounds. Times were very lawless,
cattle raiding was practised as a fine art between rival clans, and the hills
were full of broken men from various armies who lived by what prey
they could find. Seaforth, however, had to give a bond for a huge sum,
which he passed on to many of his kinsmen, including Mackenzie of
Tarbat and Mackenzie of Rosehaugh who were cautioners for the bond,
and a heavy burden it was for many years: Tarbat succeeded in borrowing
a large sum for this repayment from John Cuthbert the grain merchant
of Inverness. Middleton and Moray did not make submission until after
the Mackenzies. George Mackenzie of Tarbat undoubtedly went abroad
after this, but he was back in the later years of the Commonwealth, living
on his estates for at least part of the time, and among his papers connected
with the Union of Parliaments, fifty years later, he kept a copy of the
proclamation of the Cromwellian Protectorate of 'The commonwealth

of England, Scotland and Ireland', with his own scribbled and largely approving comments in the margin.

After this baptism of fire, Tarbat settled to the peaceful days of the Restoration, though he paid heavily for his incautious backing of Middleton, who reappeared in Scotland, high in the king's favour at first. Both Middleton and Tarbat were discredited, and Tarbat had a long haul back to royal favour.

With his record of loyalty to the house of Stuart it is remarkable that Tarbat was retained by the new King William as adviser on Highland affairs after 1688. It is still more remarkable when the rôle of his son The Master and his cousin Lord Lovat in attempting to foster a rising in Inverness to complement the rising of Dundee in Perthshire was well known, and the Master had been arrested at Tarbat House by an old family friend, Major Aeneas Mackay. His Order read:

> You are commanded to take 50 well mounted Dragoons and passing over (from Inverness) to the Shire of Ross shall labour to seize the Person of the Master of Tarbat with his two priests and papish servants as also all the armes which shall be found in his custody ... and PS seize the Master of Tarbat's serviceable horses and take a view of his papers.
> dated 11 May 1689.

By July Dundee had been killed at Killiecrankie, and soon after the remnant of his army dispersed at Dunkeld. The Master was in the Castle of Inverness for a short time and then under house arrest in Fortrose. This experience seems to have satiated his military ambitions, for he was never found in arms again. Major Mackay's wife Barbara wrote a civil letter to Lord Tarbat hoping that nothing would prevent the former friendships that had always prevailed between the two families, and later Mackay wrote in the same terms. Social life must have been difficult. Mackay himself stayed with The Master (when he had become the second Earl) and made a bid for the wrought-iron gates and statuary of Tarbat House.

The real threat of a Highland rising made the new government of King William and Queen Mary very vigilant. Colonel Hill, an old officer of Monck's campaign, was appointed to garrison the western approaches, and wrote to Tarbat on 5 July 1690 reporting progress.

> We are come safe to Lochabber and find we must garrison in the old place, there being none so conveneint tho' of itself not good ... some Palisadoes are set tho' I must expect all the mischief the rebells can do me. The preparations are short hear, being sent only 2,000 bolls of meal ...

Soon after this the garrison was renamed Fort William, in the king's honour. Col Hill wrote a number of long and interesting letters to Tarbat, dealing with the problems of the garrison (which was short of all necessities), and with the attitudes of the surrounding chiefs who had to come in and make submission to him. Eventually, before the disaster of Glencoe, Tarbat had been outmanoeuvred and had demitted office. He remained in Edinburgh, or in London, receiving a flood of letters from his estate chamberlains and his Mackenzie kinsmen who were suffering under the rule of Sheriff Ross of Balnagowan, and had to produce men for the militia, and to have troops quartered in every parish of Easter Ross. This was a heavy expense for the gentry. Tarbat himself kept a receipt from Col Cunningham, Commander in chief of their Majesties' forces in the north, who certified that the Viscount of Tarbat 'did send to Inverness upon 15 January 1692, one hundred men well armed, and clothed, with 10 days provinder'. Balnagowan's 'rule' was much resented by clan Mackenzie. On several occasions six or seven Mackenzies wrote to Tarbat 'conjointly' to report grievances. On 29 July 1689, just after Killiecrankie, Balnagowan sent a proclamation round the parishes, to be nailed to the Kirk door, to call all the Heritors to Tain to raise a Great Militia by 2 August: each Heritor owning £100 of valued rents was due to provide ten horses and one man armed and equipped. Demands for army stores were made frequently. Early in 1690 Robert Dunbar, chamberlain of Cromarty, wrote that the demand 'laid upon this shire' was for 112 bolls of meal and 3,700 stones of flour and his opposite number Meddat at Tarbat concurred that it was difficult to find. No wheat was grown there then, and flour not much in use: the troops must have been English to have expected it. By the next spring Dunbar wrote again that the 'poor tenants are much suffering through forced supply', and that Tarbat himself was at great loss through not getting payments from the Magazine in Inverness. He wrote again that the tenants were suffering losses by having to carry the impost of grain to the Magazine at Inverness, particularly as there were so few horses left, and they did not even get the money for the ferry at Kessock.

Throughout this period there are letters from Mackenzie kin in Ross to Tarbat as the most influential Mackenzie of his day: Scatwell wrote that, 'Since Balnagowan was sheriff we were scarceley the saboth this half year by-past without information at our Kirk doors desiring all men between 16 and 60 to band evryways, and it was oppressive.' Some of these commands survive. However much the Heritors suffered, the tenantry suffered more, and this was a cause of concern to the landowning class too, not entirely altruistic as their own rents were much depleted by the incessant demands of the Quartering Officers. Seven Mackenzies wrote from Kindace in 1691, following up an earlier letter, a round-robin of complaints against Balnagowan, 'Ther are some more depredations since our former letter', and Mackenzie of Ardross wrote with an example:

There is also a poore fellowe on my land in Strathensdaile who ... Balnagowan sent a partie to apprehend, not finding him they took away A poor lad that is his son and has kept him as is allowed in the place of the father this month and and more bypast in the Tolbooth of Tain where he has almost starved for want of meal and warmth ... I beg your Lordship's love to the state of affairs of this poor country.

Coull complained several times—once that he was assessed at £15. 15s. per horse quartered on him, thirteen of them, and once in more general terms. Another letter from six of the name of Mackenzie complained that they had had an unjust supply imposed on them. Hugh Dallas, the family lawyer, wrote giving another example of 'Balnagowan's men [who] will beggar the tenants of Coigach unless your lordship prevents it not, for within these two months the wage for cows was taken from a poor widow in Achashalsall, and there have been more or as many taken as before.'

The most vivid account of the misery of having troops billeted on the tenants came in several petitions. William McCulloch tenant of Pitmaduthy (Tarbat Barony) complained at the behaviour of the troops quartered on Cromartie lands at the orders of the Laird of Balnagowan who would not go until 'There was not meal or maintenance within the house'. Thomas Taylor, another tenant there was more specific; he declared upon oath that 'nyne of the same number of soldiers were quartered upon him and that he heard Balnagowan speaking in English to these soldiers and as he supposed he gave them freedom to be quartered withon doors nyne days and nyne nights ...' Taylor expended '1 boll of meal, some beer and two wedders, two hens, with butter and eggs and anything else they found upon the house.' Similar protests were made by three other small tenants. Lord MacLeod also had soldiers quartered at Castle Leod, though what they consumed is not recorded. The tenants of Pitmaduthy complained again that they were severally threatened by the sholdeiry [sic] instead of receiving any satisfaction or payment for them, and that in any case they had more, twice as many more, quartered on them than their 'nixt neighbours' and that they stayed twice as long. It certainly was the impression of the Mackenzies that Balnagowan singled them out for the worst exactions. Tarbat evidently wrote expostulating for there is a haughty reply from Balnagowan stating that all he did was in compliance with the orders of the (Privy) Council, and implying not very subtly that those who complained did not show sufficient loyalty to Their Majesties.

By the turn of the century the evil of quartering was lifting, though the hostility between Balnagowan, a convinced presbyterian and the Mackenzie kin who were not, erupted in the form of religious riots in the first decade of the eighteenth century. An attempt was also made by

Balnagowan to blacken the loyalty of all the Mackenzies who were Justices of the Peace, which was fought out even in the pages of the London newspapers with accusation and counter-accusations flying about.

Throughout the first Earl's papers there is scattered evidence of his patronage, mostly in letters asking for favours. He financed the two young Urquhart lairds whose lands he had bought, buying them commissions in the army and their uniforms, and they were not backward in asking for more. A few interesting military scraps relate to Captain John Slezar; there is a copy of his commission given by the King and Queen to be a Surveyor of the Magazines of Scotland, dated 11 January 1689. From his travels on this survey Slezar published his *Theatrum Scottica*, a book of engravings which is now of incomparable value in its depiction of the burghs of Scotland of that time. Another letter from Slezar, asking for repayment of expenses, is written by him in a beautiful hand.

In the year of his death the Earl received a letter from a niece, Margaret Munro, craving his help and protection for an army deserter, one of their tenants whom they were hiding on their property. They were fearful of his discovery and craved the Earl's help in establishing the man's freedom.

The peace of the tenantry, and of the gentry of Ross was disturbed again in 1715 when Seaforth rose and took a large contingent of Mackenzies and McCraes, 'hylanders and clannit men' with him to Sheriffmuir, and to defeat. This time the quartering was in the efficient and ruthless hands of General Wade who made Brahan Castle his headquarters in the north, and the weary round of quartering troops began again, more especially in the Strathpeffer barony which marches with Brahan.

Although none of the house of Cromartie was directly involved in the Rising of 1719, most of the clan were heavily implicated. Major-General Wade was determined to put down insurrection with a heavy hand, and some of his papers betray what would now be described as a racist attitude towards

> All and every the Clans of the Mackenzies, McRaes, Murchisons, McLays, McLennan, Mathewson, McAulay, Morrison, McLeod and all other clans or persons liable by Act of Parliament to be dis-armed: Inverness 16 August 1725.

He later noted that 'The Mackenzies and other tribes of the estates formerly belonging to the late Earl of Seaforth had given up 508 guns, 117 Broadswords 4 Targets 75 dirks and 20 pistols.' The State papers also contain letters of submission from many of the neighbouring Mackenzie lairds. Alexander Mackenzie of Dachmaluach wrote 'my estate was some time ago confiscated and sold according to Law, having nothing left but my Life and as the Clan to which I belong has peacefully delivered up their arms and I hope will be as Faithfull subjects to His Majesty King George as they have been faithful servants to their late master Seaforth', he craved pardon. Others who wrote in the same strain were George Mackenzie of Ballmuckie, an old family friend, who dated his submission from Strathpeffer, saying he had 'undergone it patiently and lived quietly, tho' very retired from the world all this time', he acknowledged his guilt. So did Roderick Mackenzie of Fairburn, and a Pardon was also granted by the king against the Attainder of George Mackenzie, son of Delvine, 'for levying war against Us within this kingdom'. The Earl of Seaforth though Attaindered was still alive and actively plotting in France though he later repented and betrayed another attempted Rising in 1727 to the Crown, hoping to get his lands thus restored. It was a period in which mutual trust must have been difficult. Seaforth's son refused to join the Rising of 1745 and commanded a regiment of Mackenzies for King George, while his cousin of Cromartie was also commanding a regiment of other Mac-kenzies for Prince Charles

The last and most disastrous of the Risings, that of 1745 had been long rumoured.

The grand enemy of England was of course France, and George II resumed operations against the old antagonist, ending for a time at the Battle of Dettingen which was a resounding English victory, and the last campaign commanded in the field by the King in person. George II was assisted by his 'army-mad' young son William Duke of Cumberland. No one doubted for a moment that this set-back to France would not result in French support for further Jacobite Risings. The third Earl heard all about this in letters from his kinsman MacLeod of MacLeod, who was sitting in Parliament, and no doubt also from his father-in-law Gordon, who was a courtier, and secretary to Frederick Prince of Wales. He kept a copy of the printed *Proceedings in Lords and Commons* of 13 February 1743, when George II sent a Royal Message 'that the eldest son of the Pretender to this Crown is arrived in France.' The message needed no gloss, though it took Prince Charles months of intrigue to get his little party together and to land in Scotland, but without the French support which was vital to success. Internal French politics had shifted away from direct help in a venture which was so dubious of success. Fifty years before, in 1698, another Royal Proclamation had warned the north to muster the Militia, as 'The French King and the implacable malice he hath on all occasions expressed against Us, our People and the Protestant religion gives us just grounds to apprehend there is an invasion intended by Bloody Papists and disaffected subjects ...' One of the provisos in this state of emergency was that all ships' masters had to carry passes, and this was of some concern to those carrying the grain shipments from Cromartie and Portmahomack, though that particular alarm came to nothing. The threat of Risings was a constant background to both government and citizenry, particularly in the Highlands, throughout this period.

Of the forty-six officers of Cromartie's Regiment in 1745 only six were not of the name Mackenzie. Many were the sons of the main landowners, and the majority came from the west. Of the men again the vast majority were clansmen, and from Coigach. Out of a force of above 200, in the final fatal engagement of this regiment outside Dunrobin Castle on the day before Culloden was fought, 178 were taken prisoner and over thirty were killed. Virtually all who survived prison conditions were transported. The work of Rev Robertson, Minister of Loch Broom, in going to the trials in Carlisle and interpreting for his Gaelic parishioners and interceding as far as he could on their behalf, was noteworthy. He even wrote giving evidence on behalf of his chief Heritor, Cromartie, then under threat of execution in the Tower of London, saying that there was most ample testimony in favour of that unhappy Lord's behaviour seven or eight years before the late Rebellion during which time he 'was the common friend and Patron of the established clergy in the North of Scotland, and did acquit him of all charge of forcing any into rebellion by letters, violence, burning of houses etc.' Robertson's testimony, over several pages, is the more striking as he never shared any Tory, episcopalian or Jacobite sentiments himself. He seems to have behaved as a disinterested Christian.

Lord John MacLeod, the Earl's eighteen year old son, was at great risk of his life as a state prisoner after the failure of the rebellion, and was also the subject of many earnest letters pleading his youth and innocence. His uncle Gordon declared in a letter to Newcastle that MacLeod had acted wholly in obedience to his father, and now

> Honours, Estate, expectancies from Birth of Public favours are all already gone. There has been a close long confinement, the further duration of which is uncertain and when it ends what remains to the Poor Boy but to push his fortune in foreign service and he goes thither loaded with a Traitor's sentence.

John MacLeod pleaded guilty, expressed contrition and was pardoned. He went to Sweden, and also served the King of Prussia, showing great military ability and gaining promotion and favours. He was also instrumental in setting up the first Masonic Lodge in Sweden—in the army— the Timbermanns Lodge, which had curious links in later years with Prince Charles Edward in exile in Rome: Prince Charles became involved in the secret world of masonry. Macleod's father the third Earl had been Grand Master of Scotland in 1743.

When John Mackenzie, Lord MacLeod, had become a Marshal in the Swedish army, loaded with honours and a veteran of numerous campaigns, his friends in Scotland tried for a long time to obtain his commission to

20 General John Mackenzie, Lord MacLeod and Count of Sweden, in full military regalia after his estates had been restored in 1784.

21   Colonel George Mackenzie of the Royal Scots and Lord MacLeod's Light
Infantry Regiment, who died in Madras when serving with the Regiment in
about 1787.

return and raise a Highland regiment for King George. Their efforts, even those of the Queen Regent of Sweden, were at first in vain, and not until 1777 did he receive a commission from George III to raise a regiment. His brother George was seconded from The Royal Scots to assist him. Recruiting methods were direct. A tenant, John McPhail of Auchterneed near Castle Leod has left a vivid picture in a petition written many years later:

> ... his father was ground-officer to the late earl of Cromartie for 40 years ... Lord Macleod wrote to John Mackenzie of Meddat from Sweden inquiring if any of the McPhails was still alive and to keep sight of them until he saw how his affairs would turn out. Colonel George sent for [me] and my wife to Castle Leod. There he wrote our names in his pocket book (and your petitioner's wife was dressing the Colonel's linens at Invergordon Castle for four years) and assured us both that if ever the estate came to Lord McLeod or his heirs they would look after us

The McPhails had been working in Skye but they returned and the engagement was honoured by Captain Kenneth, who succeeded Lord MacLeod in the estate, but he only gave them a small plot. The petition was to get a larger one. In support of the claim a postscript was added:

> Your petitioner's brother who comes along with him to wait of your honour Gave his only son to Lord McLeod how soon he came and went with him to the East Indes where his son was killed to his gret Grieff and Loss in his old age and as he labours twa lots in Ardivall side he flatters himself your honour will allow him to enjoy it in his old age.

Land hunger was so dominant that only sons were risked for the promise of a good plot. The pocket books of Corry and Col George are mentioned by several former soldiers as their security.

The Recruiting Instructions were drawn up with precision, and had eleven heads. The first stipulated that no man was to be enlisted who had stopped growing under five feet six inches, though boys under eighteen and likely to grow might be taken at five feet four inches; no man over thirty was to be enlisted, and no apprentice or collier to be enlisted. The surgeon was to examine every man. Every recruit was to be provided with three good shirts, stock and buckle, two pair Hose, Kilt, bonnet, two pair of shoes and a knapsack, the expense of which was to be taken out of his bounty money. After financial details the final item is that Officers are to keep their Parties as clean as possible and prevent them from rioting or quarrelling with Parties of other Regiments or with the inhabitants of the Place they are Quartered. There survive a few of the lists of names of recruits, all Highland names, and also the names of rejected men with the reasons given by the Surgeon. These reasons are not expressed in very clinical language: the unfortunate Alex MacDougall, aged 21, was dismissed as 'quite a miserable object', and one of 35 was 'greatly above the age'. A father and son, both called Thos. Ross, enlisted together. The Colonel of the regiment was responsible for feeding and equipping his men, and for this he went to one of the Military Agents. Once Lord MacLeod had got his regiment to Madras more documents seem to have survived. The strength of the regiment stationed at Wallajahbad on 10 September 1787 was detailed: in summary it was a Major, 4 captains, 13 lieutenants and 5 ensigns, with an adjutant and quartermaster, a surgeon, 36 sergeants, and 18 drummers and pipers, effective rank-and-file present fit for duty 642, sick present 37. With some on leave and invalids embarked for England the total was 722. At the end of that year a *General State of the Emoluments* provided a balance sheet between the Colonel and the Government. After detailing the subsidence paid, 5s. 6d. per man per day and the clothing for which allowance was made, the strength of this battalion of homesick Highlanders was 72 rank-and-file Grenadiers, 1,012 battalion soldiers and 72 Light Infantry, along with officers, NCOs and 23 pipers and drummers. The total full pay to the regiment for one day was £32. 13s. 0d. and after many calculations the Net Annual Emolument to the Colonel was a tidy £1,953. 10s. 10d. His Agent in India, Alexander Brodie at Fort St George, put in many detailed transactions, including one for pack-thread and darning thread and buttons, and for shoulder knots for uniforms. In 1781 the calculation of the numbers in the regiment showed that numbers were down; 'NB. 126 Men Prisoners with Hyder Ally not included.'

Col Lord MacLeod eventually fell out with the Company Commander-in-Chief, General Eyre Coote—there was always friction between officers of the East India Company's service, and those of the King's service drafted out to help them. Priorities were fought for the precedence meant much. MacLeod, who seems to have been a careful and considerate commander in the terms of his day, thought that the Company officers were giving his men inferior accommodation and not enough hospital facilities. He finally left his brother Col George Mackenzie in charge, and went home to claim his own estate, for which he and some hundreds of Highland enlisted men had worked so hard and long. The survivors too had earned their little plots of land.

III

Royston House
1684–1734

*The Building and Furnishings
of Royston House*

More or less as Lord Tarbat built it, the Edinburgh mansion still stands. Royston House, 'a late seventeenth century house of major importance and surprising complexity', is in the shadow the gas-holders of the city of Edinburgh, between a council estate and the cold sea. Perhaps this unfashionable location has helped to preserve it from alterations. An excellent description of the house as it was in the 1980s can be found in the Penguin *Edinburgh*, under its present name of Caroline Park, Granton.

In 1684 Sir George MacKenzie had become Viscount Tarbat in the accession honours of James II. His old rival Lauderdale was dead, and his own political progress looked assured. His Edinburgh base had been rented in Schoolhouse Wynd, apart from the short period when he and his wife occupied the accommodation in Holyrood House reserved under the Crown for the Lord Register. He needed a more permanent base and bought Royston in 1684. It was an excellent choice, and his rebuilding programme left him with a small-scale mansion of unusual design, 'half French, half Edinburgh', which will be discussed in detail later. The estate of Royston was near Granton harbour, and thus convenient for shipping from the north, but all the same it was only a short coach ride from Holyrood, Parliament House and the Royal Mile. A stoutly built tower-house, then about a hundred years old, stood on the property. Tarbat set an army of craftsmen to work on extending this tower laterally, transforming it into a sophisticated villa with an internal courtyard, stair-cases and state rooms designed to show the consequence of a great officer of State. Tarbat lived there for twenty-five years, during which time the

22   Royston House, Granton, Edinburgh, now known as Caroline Park. Another
Victorian lithograph, but more accurate than the one of Tarbat House.

north seldom saw him, although he made several visits to London. Royston was the centre of his whole estate. Lord Tarbat had made it over, in theory, to his second son, Sir James, when he had acquired the estate of Cromarty in 1684, but James was still a minor at Oxford then, and his father had no intention of giving up Royston: he retained a life-rent. James had an apartment with a private stair. He became an Advocate, and later a Lord of Session under the title of Lord Royston. He took over the property in 1712 when his father retired to Ross, taking with him two boatloads of the furnishings of Royston for the house of New Tarbat. The many family papers relating to Royston came up in the cargo to Ross, especially bunches of bills for both building and maintaining the house; pigeon-holes in the bureaux, stuffed full of them. Nowhere is there any ordered account of the household expenditure, and we may be sure that the bills which have survived are by no means the total. We have, however, Tarbat's own estimate of what the rebuilding of the house had cost him by 1705. In that year he was surviving extreme pressures from creditors brought on by his eldest son's extravagances (and some of his own). The death of his second wife and the whisper of complicity in one of the earliest Jacobite conspiracies (in 1704) had also dulled his zest for life in the city. He offered the house and the lands to his kinsman the Earl of Mar, then Tarbat's own successor as HM's Secretary of State for Scotland, to be an official residence for the Lord Chancellor of Scotland. His letter of offer reads rather like an estate agent's, and his emphasis on the difficulties of absentee governance of Scotland came from personal experience.

> For one evil in our government now is, that the Lord Chancler, beeing the first wheel in the ministry—by whose absence the government is oftymes at a stand, and at best must move unequally—[his] having the convenience of a convenient house, gardens, and parks and some rent at the door, in the seat of government with excellent healthful situation, takes away pretence of going to his country, tho' perhaps at a distance, or rather will invite the succeeding Chanclers to stay more fixedly at the helm.

Tarbat calculates optimistically that the surrounding land will provide 'at worst ... 12 chalders at £1,200 Scots constant rent, and £80 Sterling of money rent for the parks' (i.e. £960 Scots) making a total of £2,160 Scots ... 'Now for the building', he continues, 'I value it willingly a third less than it cost, or less than it were possible to build it, that is £4,000 Sterling, (£48,000 Scots) and I can swear it cost me six.' Tarbat concludes his letter with suggesting the added advantage that the Lord Chancellor of Scotland need not be paid £200 (Scots) of his current salary if such handsome accommodation were to be provided for him. Mar's refusal of this offer is lost: the map of fashionable Edinburgh never included Granton, nor did the Chancellor acquire lodgings there—it seems a pity.

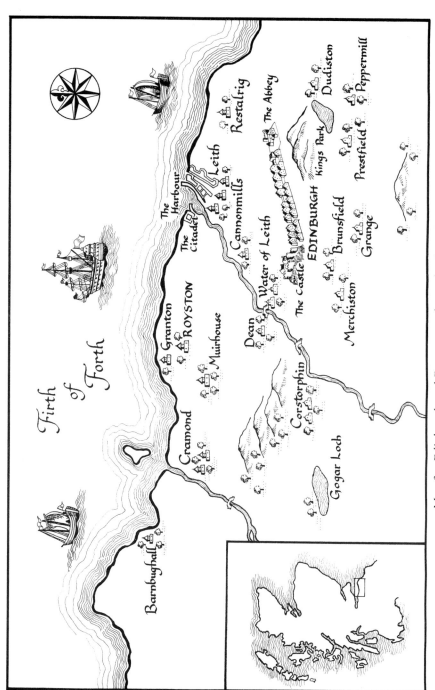

Map 3   Edinburgh and Royston, redrawn by Janet Ross.

James, Lord Royston survived there to an old age, but the estate of Royston was sold by his heirs in 1734. The new owner was the 2nd Duke of Argyll, who in compliment renamed the house Caroline Park, after his daughter, and the Hanoverian Queen. Argyll employed Robert Adam to put in a few new fireplaces, and a range of stabling, but the house was little used and for generations was let to a succession of Edinburgh worthies, until the gasworks were built in late Victorian times so near as to render it useless for polite occupation; for many years the office of a commercial ink-works occupied the building. Royston is now being revived; North Sea gas no longer smells, nor does the proximity of the densely-built council estate offend, as it did a generation or two ago. Royston—Caroline Park—has long awaited a sensitive re-developer.

During the twenty-five years of Lord Tarbat's occupation his career, both public and private suffered many of the swooping changes of fortune which always characterised it. During the reign of James II Tarbat was in high favour, Secretary of State and a leader of Edinburgh society. He was involved in the foundation of the Royal College of Physicians of Scotland in 1680, he was a convivial host and party guest, entrusted by the King with the setting up of the revived Order of the Thistle, and by his peers with the colourful office of Captain General of the Royal Company of Archers. Then came the revolution of 1688. The temperate rejoicing for the birth of the first son to the King on June 10 was hardly over in Edinburgh before news came that the Whig nobles of England had conspired to evict him and his Catholic queen and their infant son, and to bring William of Orange over from Holland. William was an impeccable Protestant, married to James' own elder daughter, Mary, who was also Protestant. The Revolution was called 'glorious' in England; in Scotland there was more sorrow at the putting-down of one of the house of Stuart. Though James' Romish tendencies were deeply deplored, he was of the old blood, and even presbyterian divines quoted Holy Writ about the 'right of the first-born son', and the fate of evil dispossessors.

Tarbat was one of the Assembly which, in the absence of a ruler to call a parliament, sat to hear the rival claims of James, erstwhile king, and William, putative king, to the crown of Scotland. James wrote them a snarling note demanding obedience and affirming the Divine Right of Kings. William wrote a quieter affirmation, promising nothing but his continued adherence to the Protestant faith. Scotland voted for William, and quite soon Lord Tarbat was recalled to the service of the Crown, as adviser on Highland affairs. No one, it was thought, knew the Highlands better: the relationships, the network of indebtedness, obligation and kinship which linked the great Highland families. It was true, and the plans put forward by Tarbat had some chance of reconciling the chiefs to the rule of King William, as the main plank of his scheme was to offer some protection of these families, in the name of the Crown, against the inroads of Clan Campbell, then in highly expansionist mood. This naturally antagonised Clan Campbell, and after the customary covert intrigues at William's court of Kensington, Tarbat was displaced and Campbell of Breadalbane took over. Tarbat's poor muddled old friend, Col Hill, Commander of Fort William, and veteran of Cromwell's New Model Army, was soon sending out a detachment of Campbells to police the village of Glencoe. Tarbat himself at this point was seriously ill, though the nature of his illness is not recorded. His friends, who include most of the Edinburgh College of Physicians and some eminent London practitioners, wrote copious and contradictory letters of advice. Even his bookseller in London sent congratulations when he recovered (together with his account for the expensive books ordered by Tarbat's son John). In 1699 Tarbat's wife Anna Sinclair took ill, and some of her sufferings until her death are mentioned in an earlier chapter. Tarbat seemed crushed by her loss, but like many widowers he did not take long to find another wife. This was Margaret, Dowager Countess of Wemyss. Tarbat, who by then was nearly seventy, treated his bride with the enthusiasm of a much younger groom. He redecorated the apartments at Royston which his former wife had used, he added more baroque touches to the house, and gave her lavish presents including clothes, furs and wigs and a full dressing-set of silver. Fortunately an upward swing in his political fortunes enabled the newly married pair to go to London where they made several long stays. They also made visits to the lady's son, the Earl of Wemyss, in Fife, where Tarbat interested himself in the coal mines which were David Wemyss' chief preoccupation. Characteristically he took over and organised barley exports from the estate. Tarbat's mother came from Fife and he had a ready-made circle of friends and kin there too. The sister of Margaret Countess of Wemyss and Tarbat, was the celebrated 'ABC', Anne Countess of Buccleuch and Cornwallis, formerly the wife of Monmouth, who had challenged King James and lost his head. She and her sister were always close, and her portrait came to Royston along with her sister's. The correspondence holds quite a few rather imperious letters from ABC to Lord Tarbat on business and political affairs. Several other ladies wrote to him for help and advice, particularly widows with recalcitrant sons, though Tarbat's own record as a parent was not, one would have thought, one to emulate. Tarbat's happiness with his second wife did not last. She died of a rheumatic fever on one of their visits to London in 1705. Elaborate mourning, suitable for so great a lady, with all the trappings of the age was carried out, in London, Edinburgh and finally in Wemyss where she was buried. Tarbat composed a Latin epitaph for a memorial; he also commissioned a lead monument, half life size, with *putti* and mourning angels to be sculptured by Rysbrach. Paying for all this added very much to the financial stringency begun in 1704, the year when John's creditors banded together to put pressure on the estate. This was also a year of major events of more widespread importance. King William died in London, and ex-King James died in France. Queen Mary had long predeceased William and the succession went to her sister, Queen Anne, the other Protestant daughter of the dead James II.

Tarbat must have known the Princess Anne well when her father was Duke of York and came to live in Holyrood in the 1670s. Although Tarbat was an old man, by the time she came to the throne, she sent for him, created him an Earl in her accession honours, and made him Secretary of State for Scotland. He had a late flowering as Queen Anne's Secretary, though as usual there were ups and downs. The great question of the day in Scotland (England's interest was tepid) was the possibility of the Union of Parliaments. The old Earl was an enthusiastic promoter of the Union; he wrote many speeches and published pamphlets on this topic. His arguments were almost wholly economic, he saw that Scotland was small and under-capitalised, relying on minor exports of primary products such as salt, fish, skins and raw wool, whereas English exports of manufactured goods to Europe were well-established and permitted return imports of luxuries as well as staple needs (such as French wine, the timber of Norway and iron of Sweden). Scotland could not afford either staples or luxuries, but once the customs' barriers at the Border were removed, and Scotsmen could join the East India Company, the Hudson Bay Company and trade to America and the West Indies, the country's future would be, he hoped, assured. In strictly economic terms of course he was right, but his enthusiasm for the new Great Britain—the term had just come into favour—blinded him to the loss of identity and of nationhood which Scotland was to suffer from Union. The massive long-lasting indifference of the English to Scottish national, political and economic problems compounded the hurt, but were not foreseen by him. The Union was signed in May 1707. The Earl remained at Royston for another five years. He was not alone. His son James seems to have made his home at Royston, and at some point the old Earl took a mistress. Her name was Frances Walker: she seems to have been a gentlewoman and accepted socially by his old cronies. She may have had some connection with one or other of his wives as, after his death when his youngest daughter was trying to evict her, Mistress Walker writes sentimentally, claiming (amongst a great many other goods) 'the portrait of my late dear Lady'.

When Tarbat first rebuilt Royston, he used the north end facing the sea as the main entrance with a new façade with two rather oddly shaped dutch gables which bore a long Latin verse written by himself. This verse must have caused wry faces as the many creditors of the estates made their way in. It reads in translation:

Riches unemployed are of no use; but made to circulate they are productive
of much good. Increase of property is accompanied by a corresponding
increase of care. Wherefore for their own comfort and that of their friends
George and Ann Viscount Tarbat have caused this small cottage to be built
in the Christian era, year 1685. Enter our guests, for this is a house of
entertainment; now it is ours, soon it will be another's, after our death whose
we neither know nor care, for none has a certain dwelling place.

Therefore let us live well while we may.

The original building, hardly a cottage, lay to the west, a short L-shape
which was converted into two wings of the courtyard quadrangle. The
ground plan, and the lay-out of the first floor echoes in miniature the
grandest contemporary buildings such as Panmure House and Kinross
House. The architect is unknown, though the influence of Tarbat's old
friend Sir William Bruce is clear. There also exists a bond for a large sum
of money due to Sir Robert Mylne, though there is no evidence of it
being a payment for services rendered. The north front with its odd gables
and the Latin inscription panel (which looks as if a monumental mason
had been diverted from a gravestone to set its flourishes) is really rather
provincial and clumsy. Tarbat learned fast, however, for a few years later
he turned the axis of the house round, and made a new entrance façade
at the south aspect of the new quad. This is a marvellously successful
composition; John Gifford aptly wrote: 'the South front is without parallel
in Scotland, the general outline is French, the detail Edinburgh'. The two
end-pavilions have ogee roofs reminiscent of many of Bruce's buildings,
but the very strong rustication and strongly-defined ashlars, and the small
square cupolas do have a French feel. The date carved over the lintel is
1693, and Tarbat's name and that of his first wife Anne are blazoned on
each of the end corner towers. It was built partly because the existing
south entrance was unsatisfactory, and partly because the local inhabitants
continued to use as a right-of-way the garden path by the shore line. On
entering by the new South front doorway—it certainly looks as if an
external sweep of steps to take the visitor up to the first floor was intended
but never implemented—the visitor had to walk through an anteroom
and across the courtyard to the north entrance hall where an ornate staircase
took him to the first floor. The wrought iron work of the stair balustrades
is light and elegant, with roses and scrolls of great delicacy. There is foliage
everywhere, on the landing in wood and iron work, and on the ceilings
of the state apartments in plaster. Borders of oak-leaves and of bay leaves
surround coroneted monograms and rather turgid paintings. (The paintings may date, however, from the next owner's occupation.) The fireplaces
in the smaller rooms are placed across the corners of the anterooms, in the
Restoration manner, with tiered shelves in the plaster above, designed for

the display of blue-and-white china, which was the craze of the day for Williamites—either the expensive imports from China or the Delft copies from Holland. Tarbat almost certainly had both kinds, including 'four flower potts' which were probably the Tulip pots favoured by Queen Mary, delft pyramids or obelisks, five foot or more from the floor on which their solid bases stood, with cupped niches for the display of tulips, all the way up.

From the Inventar of furnishings of Royston dated 2 April 1703 a vivid picture of the household can be gained. Downstairs, at the north entrance are listed the Kitchen, wash-house, and then the Withdrawing room and dining room; from their rather perfunctory furnishings this is where the servants, the clients and the outright hangers-on were accommodated and fed. The Parlour next to the Porter's Lodge had only two oval tables, a dozen cane chairs and a grate with shovel and poker, tongs and a fender. It is a careful and detailed inventory. Up the staircase the visitor would pause only to note two glass hanging lanthorns and three pictures before arriving at the Upper Dining Room, which however seems to have been furnished more as a gallery or waiting room with 'A Japan table and stand, 15 of La Brun's Prints in frames, three maps in frames, the palace and city of Naples in frames, 8 black cane chairs and a large oval table.'

The Upper Withdrawing room, listed next, is a gracious room with a dozen chairs covered in green velvet 'and silver stuff' with tapestry hangings, large looking-glasses, glass sconces for wall candles and a quantity more of the Japan furniture in black lacquer, including a pair of chests on stands, a Japan tea table, and 'a large walnut-tree desk'. Queen Anne was not yet on the throne: it was the height of fashion.

The Bedchamber had a state bed, a four-poster with bunches of ostrich feathers at the corners (called Tour-de-loos) and curtains of red paragon. The furnishings were to match. There were two other bed-chambers, one containing the Holyrood state bed hung in green, and 'Mr James' chamber' rather modestly furnished, but including 'four leather chairs' for the entertainment of his friends in private perhaps. His father's closet, identified with one of the small rooms on the east corner of the house, with its little private staircase in a turret to the ground floor, and a postern door, has a 'walnut tree desk' and 'a table cover'd wt. green baize'. This inventory does not list any of the rooms on the other side of the courtyard assigned to Lady Tarbat, and then to the Countess of Wemyss.

Five years later an even fuller Inventar was taken in which we can recognise various items from the earlier lists. In The Closet of My Lord's Bedchamber, for example, he now has the chairs 'with silver stuff' and the maps which were in the waiting room, and which turn out to be maps of 'Great Britain, Terra Sanola [Hispanola?] and Gallia [France]'. He had a large picture of Lady Tarbat in a gilt frame—his first wife. He used

books of reference: 'Ane Oxford Almanack' was handy, and several lamps
and candlesticks. On his desk, the same walnut one, was

> a Brass lamp rising and falling on a brass stalk, a white-iron lamp, a reading
> glass on a brass stalk ... a japanned coffie pot, a copper coffie pot, a copper
> chaffer ... a thea japann'd table with a china thea pot and a china basin, eight
> different cups ... (on the hearth) a pair of long shovels coal axe and hearth
> brush. The room hung with stripped Musselborough stuffe.

It sounds comfortable and practical.

By this time his second wife was dead and his daughter the Lady Anne
lived with him, as well as his youngest son James. Lady Anne had another
complete tea equipage, with 'six china cups and saucers conform'—not
odd ones as her father's six seem to have been—and she slept in a 'throne
bed with blew stuff curtains lined with a copper silk, fringed'. By this
time also Mrs Walker was installed, with a small sitting room nicely
furnished. She seems to have had a taste for the highly fashionable black
japan lacquer furniture: 'a fine japanned cabinet wt. raised work, on a
gilded carved standish, a little cabinet above the big one', and a bedroom
with 'a large looking-glass, a standing bed with green silk curtains and
three pairs of blankets, feather-bed and bolsters and a tartan quilt'. Winters
can be cold down by the shore in Edinburgh. She also had a black japanned
tea-table and a number of other furnishings of some luxury. All the rooms
were supplied with necessities: 'a close box, and pan, a lime chamber-pot
and a basin'.

This inventory was taken by the chaplain, Mr Roy Mathesone, and
'writt at Royston 8 October 1708' and is signed as correct by George Earl
of Cromartie.

Many of the furnishings so carefully inventoried are recognisable in the
two ships' cargoes taken north in 1712. The walnut writing cabinets, the
four Arras hangings, and the black jappaned lacquer chests-on-stands
reappear until the last Roup, the auction of the furnishings of Castle Leod
and of New Tarbat after the grandson of Earl George had been attained
and forfeited for rising in support of Prince Charles Edward. In a small
farmhouse today, near Alness, there is one battered black jappaned cabinet,
of the right period, which it is tempting to think *might* just have been one
of those sold in the Roup of New Tarbat. The present elderly owner only
knows that his great grandfather bought it in some big house-sale. All of
the present furnishings of the family of Cromartie that can certainly be
dated back three hundred years are the family portraits (including that of
Lady Tarbat which her husband kept in his closet), and all the family
papers, not only the Charters and Bonds of generations, but the bills for
the baker and the flesher who kept the family supplied in Royston, and
all the other ephemera which have been used to build up this picture.

The estimate that the first Earl made, that Royston had cost him 'above £6,000 sterling', that is £72,000 Scots, is impossible to verify now: all the same one suspects that at no point did the owner count the cost, or draw up neat accounts. Certainly we have found none. His offer to sell the house to the state was first made in 1705 and repeated six or so years later. Marr did not respond favourably. The term 'architect' had hardly come into currency, and the papers are no help. Sir Robert Mylne of Blackburn Kt registered a Bond for £2,800 owing to him by Tarbat in 1698: ten years before he had given him a receipt of £45 sterling (£660 Scots), but whether these were for services or as a loan between gentlemen is not clear: the same goes for several Bonds with Sir William Bruce, a close friend. The chief workman at Royston seems to have been Alexander Eizatt, who not only was paid (comparatively small amounts) but receipted delivery of sundries such as slates, nails, deals and lead. His wife occasionally signed for him. Lime and cut stones were delivered by sea, some from South Queensferry and Hopetoun, and a carter was paid to carry up from the shore. Some of the specialist bills are interesting: John Witterlie, slater, made a contract to supply and maintain the slates for Royston and of the new house at School Wynd, and to harle the latter, in 1688. Although there was a hint of an indefinite contract, several other slaters are mentioned, and by 1706 one Peter Simpson, slater-burgess of Canongate, successfully sued for payment of £400 Scots. Some plumbers drift through the record. Cornelius Jackson 'of London', plumber, must have been in Edinburgh at some time as he records that he had borrowed £22 Scots from James Haig, gardener at Royston. Although the names of several smiths and metal-workers occur, no smith is given the prominence that the maker of the main balustrade of the staircase deserves, and the now lost gateway with its head was probably of excellent quality too. Mostly the amounts are trivial: 'James Frier, Smith without the Watergate', was, for example, paid £16. 4s. 6d. 'in full', and some smiths are also classed as farriers, shoeing horses. Another small account was settled for Alexander Thorburn upholsterer, in 1707, for £15 Scots. The newly created Earl of Cromartie paid £100 Scots to Captain Walter Milvill, Herald Painter in Edinburgh— for blazons and registered coats of arms. One of them may have been the boldly executed coat of arms of Sir Kenneth Mackenzie and his wife, as Laird of Cromarty, painted on wood panel which were found in the kirk loft of Cromarty in the 1960s.

By 1712, when the old Earl was contemplating his retreat to the Highlands, he made an agreement with his son James, by then Lord Royston, a Lord of Session. James was 'to enjoy Royston and have right to possess', but fairly extensive reservations were made: the Earl was to have use and possession of the east half of the mansionhouse 'from south to north the stairs and passages, also the Easter pavillion in the garden', and a number

23 Sir James Mackenzie, third son of the first Earl in his robes as Lord Royston, High Court of Session Judge.

of specified outhouses including 'the washing house with the stable-court and room for a coach, and the new orchard, and the little one'. The Earl paid his son £80 Scots yearly of rent for this, and there is a hint of reluctance to leave at all. It was maliciously reported that he planned to live frugally in Ross for six years until he could afford another trip to London. But the old Earl was over eighty, he did not have six years more; his course was run.

The Gardens of Royston

No lay-out remains among the family papers to indicate the extent and plan of the gardens of Royston in Tarbat's day, and nothing remains on the ground. There are a number of tantalising references, nearly all in letters exchanged between George the first Earl and his youngest son James who lived with him at Royston and inherited it, taking the title of Lord Royston when he became a Lord of Session in 1710.

As early as 1687, soon after his acquisition of Royston, Tarbat wrote to an old friend, Reverend James McLellan, Minister of Fearn Abbey in Easter Ross, on kirk affairs, adding a postscript to the letter:

> I pray you if you find any occasion by sea, send me as many willows and sahels for setting as you can conveniently ... meanwhile send me by post some little bundle of privot, sarh, great short setts of it.

The only possible deduction is that Royston garden was being planted out at the same time as Tarbat garden, and there was a shortage of the hedging plants of privet and willow. Two different spellings of the more familiar *Saugh*, the Scots for willow, may indicate different kinds of willow—there are several native dwarf kinds in the north—or may just mean the writer was in a hurry.

Later the New Tarbat gardener was asked to send cuttings for hedges at Royston. There is good evidence that the garden had a pavilion and terraces. A recurring item was 'stones for pavement', and these were laid down outside the house as well as within the central courtyard, where they still remain. James Wood, Quarrier in Queensferry, was paid £15. 16*s*. Scots for '9 score and ten stones for the pavement to the forecourt at Royston' in August, 1703. William Wright in the same year put in his bill for laying them:

49 days lebelling the forecourt	£19	06	08 Scots
6 days an borrollman at the well stair	2	00	00
3 days worke at the putting of hay to the Loft	1	00	00
2 days worke at the gairnel in the yaird	0	13	04
Summa	£23	00	00

There are several other references to the ships bringing in paving stones from Queensferry. The reference to the Girnel house is the only one located so far, indicating that part of the trade in bere from Ross actually passed through the yard of the great house.

Alexander Eizatt, the master mason, took delivery of 103 stones of bere 'for the use of the Viscount Tarbat at Royston', just after the house was bought. It is no longer clear where the well which William Wright mentions in his bill was located. Wright presented his accounts in old fashioned merks Scots.

Later a garden pavilion, and wrought-iron work to the well-head, and elaborate iron-work gates can be inferred from fragmentary references. The only letter which is clearly about the garden is one from James Mackenzie to his father in London, written from Royston in April 1711:

> The anemonies your lordship sent downe last harvest were not carefully dried and so were mouldy and tho' they were sett according to the precise rules proscribed by the author of *The Retired Gardiner* yet barely one out of six came up, of these few some are the single. I sett at the same time a parcel I had from Holland which thrive verie well ... and as also some verie good ranunculus for which I was obliged to my Lord Lyon, my master in gardening. The jonquills your lordship sent down hold very well but the narcissus are verie Common, most being the common Daffadilly. Its probable before you leave London the season of buying more anemonies and Ranunculus and Tuberoses and Tulips etc., may come. Double Auriculars and stript are not to be had except the red and yellow, its a pritty flower, hardy and multiplies fast. I am not for verie costly or very dear flowers. If your lordship would ask from the Bishop of London a sett of the Tulip Tree of which he has several it might be put in a pott and sent by sea, it is a great curiosity, and all propagate from the famous tree in my Lord Peterborough's garden at Parson's Green.

April in the garden at Royston in 1711, with the stone walls complete, sheltering, perhaps, a planting of 'the new small orchard' with those troublesome anemonies, the rampant auriculas and the common daffadilly all a-blow in the east wind of the Lothian coast, must have been beautiful. James is the most sympathetic of the Tarbat children of his generation. By 1711 he was nearing forty, and was married to one of his Rosehaugh cousins. A few months later, with his father still in London, he wrote a long gossipy letter in which he said, 'None of our seed merchants have sweet bay berries or any flowering shrub to sell, so I wish your lordship would send downe a few by hand.' To grow sweet bay, or tuberoses in the vicinity of Leith now would be quite an achievement: to contemplate it in 1711 is sophisticated gardening. We know even less about the gardeners at Royston than about the Froggs of Tarbat. Several are mentioned.

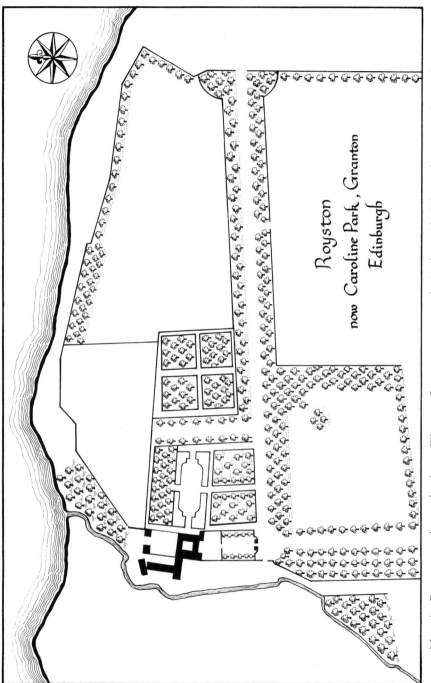

Map 4 Royston, redrawn by Janet Watson, from a survey made in the mid eighteenth century by William Edgar. Original in the possession of the Duke of Buccleuch and reproduced with his permission.

Royston

now Caroline Park, Granton

Edinburgh

'James Brown, Gardener and his two men at £120 Scots figure in the Poll Tax return of 1694. Alexander Colterd, gardener is paid a high wage of £43 *sterling* by James Mackenzie in 1709, adding £5 sterling for a half year in 1710, and 48 shillings for his expenses. He has not been traced elsewhere.

The links with the Royal College of Physicians of Scotland have been remarked on. The head gardener of the College of Physicians borrowed a small amount of money from Charles Kinross of Royston, the Earl's secretary, underlining the friendly ties.

Royston: the Household

The household bills have only survived in a random way, but there are a number for Royston days, possibly because the Earl employed a good secretary, Charles Kinross, and possibly because the chest or writing desk where the papers were amassed was whisked out of the reach of the occupying soldiers of King George in 1746 by the diligent factor Mackenzie of Meddat. The survival of any documents dating from before the upheaval of the Forty-five is remarkable; the survival of fragile scribbles from the shopkeepers of Edinburgh, the milk bill or the bakers' account, is really remarkable.

> John Moffat, Candlemaker in Musselburgh gives receipt for £30. 8. 0 Scots for the price of 10½ stone of candles. 1706
> In the same year George Mackfarling Candlemaker-Burgess of Edinburgh was paid £110 Scots.

In 1700 a Hogshead of Wine was bought for £14 *sterling* with an explanatory note that it was 'brought over in year 1695'. It was a tremendous price. The same supplier sold 14 lb. sugar candy. Two years later the Countess of Wemyss was billed for £36 sterling for wines, in part payment, from Helen Cook, spouse to G Kendall, Vintner in Leith. Claret was the preferred drink of the Scots upper class and the links with French exporters was a long-standing one, going back to James IV's days. The wine importers from Bordeaux also sent loadings of Atlantic sea-salt which was much in demand as the best salt for the Scots salmon-curing business. At this point, when England (but not Scotland) was at war with France, French wines were banned from England—not a great hardship as the English palate was more used to the heavier wines of Portugal and Spain, port, sherry or sack. It looks, however, as if the earl intended selling the French wine in London. But fine wines were not the only drink appreciated. In 1703 there is a receipt for a carrier of Berwick for £14. 12s. Scots, for the carriage of English Ale to Royston for the use of George Viscount Tarbat.

Round about the turn of the century the Earl was deeply concerned in the Leith Glass Company, whose aim was to supply green glass bottles to vintners and to apothecaries throughout Scotland at a cheaper rate than English imported bottles. The venture eventually failed, but all the Cromartie properties can be identified by cellars full of green glass bottles, if by nothing else. They were imported by the shipload to Ross. In 1704 24 dozen chopin bottles were received by Charles Kinross, the secretary, from the Leith company 'to fill wine for London'. This may have been that hogshead of old French wine or another Leith import, which either for sale or for putting on his lordship's table, was better value than any easily found in London.

Small bills were sent in by pastry cooks, and by Macmillian, Flesher-Burgess of Edinburgh, for flesh supplied to the household, and by Michael Wauch 'for all milk supplied to his lordship's family' in 1703.

The kitchen at Royston was, judging by the inventories, vastly better equipped than those in the north. The list of kitchen gear has more than forty items, with another long list of household china in 'The Pantrie and Cupboard'. The kitchen gear included several stewing dishes, pots with lids, and a dozen of pewter dishes and 8 assets (serving plates), together with all the jacks and chains for roasting before the fire, a series of kitchen knives, and a large marble mortar with a timber pestle. The butler's pantry held much predictable stuff, and his cellar, perhaps also predictably held 'ten dozen of chapkin bottles and eleven dozen of muchkin bottles'.

There are also lists of brushes and cleaning materials in what we would now call the housemaids' broom cupboards, and a room called The Womens' House where the laundry was done, contained 'a long fir table for the dressing of linens, and a fir screne for the drying of laundry, two pairs of smooth irons and a standard and hearth ...'

Two fragments of manuscript cookery books have survived. Neither are dated, but the shorter, just four pages with delicious ideas for cooking a clear red currant jelly and other desserts, is in the writing of the beginning of the seventeenth century, and in fact looks more English than Scots of that date. It has been torn out of a book, and we will never retrieve its history now. The other is much more of a working set of recipes for a cook in a large establishment, rather an old-fashioned one by the date Cromartie lived at Royston. It is not dated and the handwriting and spelling is clear though the spelling of 'flour' fluctuates. There are over fifty recipes, mostly for pies, in the early Stuart or Tudor manner. There are many standard recipes for 'coffin pies'. For example: '*salmond py*: butter it well, strow it with pepper and salt a little fresh herbs strown small, liquor it with vinnegar and oil'. Cold pigeon pie, oyster, calves' foot, mutton, lamb and blackcock were all treated in the same way. The 'coffin'—a term which was both expressive and descriptive—was the basic deep pastry case for all show dishes. '*A chikon py*: butter your chikons well, strow them over with grossets (gooseberries) in summer and currans in winter, liquor your py wt. wine'. For *A Date Py* you are instructed to 'make ready puff paste if you will'; as for the dates: 'put them below on the bottom of your py, then a row of apples, then a row of dates, then a row of apples with ambergris, cannol and nutmeg and ginger. Sugar it well, liquor with wine rosewater'. It is hard to believe that this was not overdone. Cannol was cinnamon. *A Set-up Custard* sounds more appealing: 'Take a mutchkin of fresh cream, twelve yolks of eggs well beat, a little rosewater, sugar and cannol. Let the custard be half-beaten, then let put in your liquor and when it is beaten then strew it and envelop it in sugar and cannol'. It would have made a stiff and rich pudding. Not till number twenty-five does this cook describe the making of *puff pastry*: not much changed over the centuries: 'Take a fourget of flower, kned into it two eggs and a littel rosewater and clear well water together, then roll it out wt a rolling pinn, put in fflour pieces and lay little bills of butter on every piece, strowing a little flower above your butter, laying every piece above another and rolling it again wit your rolling pin, and doe it five or sic tymes and then roll it out and make it conform to your plate whaairon put anything you please'.

The fact that this cook writes 'whaairon' and of 'a grosset tairt' for a gooseberry tart ('and a cherry tairt is made the same way') convinces us that he or she was a Scot; in that 'tairt' there are echoes of Edinburgh. The emphasis in many receipts on 'clear well water' reminds us how easily dishes might be tainted by impure water. For 'your coffins' he recommends something like a hot-water crust, perhaps the ancestor of the famous mutton-pies of Scotland whose pastry is so plain and strange to foreigners from England or France. 'One pound of butter to one peck of flour, prettie stiff, water scalding hot, and put it one hour with your leaven, make up your coffins and dry them in the oven before you fill them'. To make French bread he recommends that you 'Take 15 eggs to half a peck of fflour and cast them with sweet milk and a little barm (yeast) beat all together: mind to warm your milk a little, make small truncheons of bread, mind to take out half your whites if you would have them light'.

The most elaborate receipt is for *Chresmess Cake*, but the result of the complicated instructions would be more like a very rich Black Bun than a present-day cake. Lacking a cake-tin, you were instructed to make it in 'a coffin of greasy paper' (greaseproof-paper), and when cooked it was to be glazed with sugar and replaced in the oven to harden the glazing and it will be as white as milk'. *Wiggs* are another classic Scots small biscuit, along with shortbread, which can be passed with desserts made with 'Ryce milk, apple cream, or hanged cream (in a linen bag)'. This is what would now be sold as *crême frais*. He served it with sugar, fruit, and cream 'and to remember to garnish milk dishes with sprigs or knobs of flowers or roses and laikwise to strow them above with sugar'.

We do not know who the writer was. All the cooks whose wages occasionally appear in the accounts were men. In the Poll Tax of 1694 the cook is not identified, but other sources suggest that he is the lowly-paid Nicholas Montgomery on £24, and having to find his own £4 for 'the cook's man on the cook's fee'. The apprentice man would help with the preparation and clearing of such meals. The directions, lavish with cream and eggs as they are, should be approached carefully by modern cooks bent on reconstruction. Where Nicholas Montgomery and his fellow cooks refer to 'a pint of cream' they refer to a Scots pint, which was approximately double the quantity of an imperial pint. No wonder attempts to unify the measures of England and Scotland were so unpopular, and had to wait for the fierce legislation of 1824.

Amongst the duties of the Butler was the safe custody of the family silver, and general oversight of the household goods. The office of House-keeper does not seem to have been filled by a woman in the Royston household; it was the butler who countersigned inventories, and saw to the goods. The women servants of all the households seem to have been secondary, to a surprising degree. Probably one of the men servants was Lord Tarbat's body-servant (or valet in later terminology). He had a busy and responsible job, maintaining and packing all the finery necessary to a great officer of state, from the sky-blue silk suit with stockings and silver garters to match to the comfortable knitted nightcaps and quilted dressing-gown for relaxation at night. Some of the lists were clearly made out by Lord Tarbat himself, or altered by him. In this matter at all events he was a most careful, perhaps pernickety, person. His equipment was as showy as his clothes, and as carefully listed.

A separate Inventar deals with the period, about 1680, when Tarbat, as Lord Register had an apartment in 'The Abbay of Holyrudehouse, My lord's bedchamber' as the list has it. This was the royal palace, neglected since James VI's court went south eighty years before, but refurbished by Sir William Bruce at royal command, after the Restoration. Bruce and Tarbat were related by the marriage of Tarbat's eldest daughter to David Bruce. In Holyrood are several articles of furniture which are afterwards identifiable elsewhere:

> Ane shewed bed of silk and worsett wt. tour-de-loo of green stuff and four worsett knoupes wt one matt below the bed value £960 Scots.

This is the only inventar with valuation included. The chief interest in it, beside the first appearance of the Green Show Bed, with its ornamental tufts of feathers and the braided knots at the corners is the three pieces of Arras, here valued at £553. 6s. 8d. Scots, and the first appearance of the

tee table
tee pot, 7 cuppes,
7 sauces, (saucers)
1 boteell
and ye sugardish being ye sett for ye table ...
The best large flower pot,
ane eboyne walnut tree table, £15;
and ane pendulum clock £144.
Two little bease groupes

This last item may refer to the bronze (?) statue of hares, elsewhere called 'two rabbetts', in later lists. The list for Holyrood is the first one for which a list of silver survives:

4 silver tankers, 2 raised, 2 plain
3 poringers
2 salts giben to Collin Mackenzie
2 salvers plain
2 rings for ashetts [rings to keep hot dishes from marking a table]
2 silver sconces in my Ladies chamber in Edinburgh
2 dizen of silver [trunikers?] whereof one dizen giben in to the Minthous.
a pair of silver sconces in the drawing room at Edinburgh
three jappanned silver flower potts verie slight
ane tass of silverworke raised and gilded being the onlie peice of old plate remaining in the hous.
two of the above porringers, the one having a cover, given in with the salts and some silver works of my Ladies, to Mr Mackenzie.
the above dizan old spoons also given in to Mr Mackenzie
Ane dizen of new spoons
Ane pare of new candlesticks, wt snuffers and box conform
ane new chaffer.
                              signed: Tarbat

nota: two of the tankers given by my wife to my daughter Tarbat, the rest belong to my wife and me during lyfe and to her if she survive me.

The interesting feature of this list is that it records the time when the Mint of Scotland was so reduced that several of the great officials of state had to contribute their own house-silver to be coined to maintain the coinage of the realm.

   Part of the Holyrood Inventar of 1693 alludes also to the Palace of Linlithgow, and records other furnishings of value, and 'silber worke' of which the most valuable is 'ane large gilded Caisson', with its weight given, valued at £305, and '3 silver casters, the one for sugar, the oy. for vinegar and ye 3rd for mustard'. A number of spoons, forks and candlesticks of various kinds make up the total. The Caisson was not a gilded wooden Florentine Cassone: it was a casket weighing 405 drams, 8 drops, which might work out at nearly a pound and a half, about 750 grammes. A second list, dated 1700, covers almost identically the same silver items. Two lists of clothes for 1691 and for 1692 are mainly in Lord Tarbat's own hand, and are very similar. He lists garments in a 'selak' trunk, an article of luggage which makes many appearances. It was probably made of sealskin. In 1692 anyhow it contained worn clothes:

> a suit of flour'd velvet black with coat and black velvet breeches Filamort velvet breeches, Filamort stiff coat
> Woven breeches, a pr. buff breeches, an old black quilted justicar [and five others, all described, and some more breeches]

In another chest:

> 6 flannin shirts with flannin sleeves, 10 flannin shirts wt caligo sleeves; ... holland wastcoats, woven linen wastcoat, flannin wastcoat, spare sleeves and drawers, 10 of knit nighthoods ... [and much else]

On 10 July 1693, the same day as the silver and furniture at Holyrood was listed, a number of clothes were also delivered to George Mackenzie at Royston. It sounds as if Lord Tarbat was then finally flitting out of Holyrood into his own house of Royston.

> *The linens and other cloths delivered*:
> Muslin ruffs 5 pair
> 15 of plain gravats [cravats]
> of porrit gravat
> of lawn ruffs 7 pr.
> underclothes 6
> linen nightcaps 4
> nighthoods 4
> one stitched lawn nightcap
> [and so on through holland sleeves, handkerchiefs and drawers]

The clothes list for the same date goes on with shoes, slippers and riding boots, a 'shaven cloth and razor check, a razor, two barbers' [bowls] a spunge, a basin.'

The other clothes are much like the list of two years earlier, except for new best wear. The colour copper was the year's colour: 'Ane coper-coloured coat with vest and breeches', and another 'coper-coloured coat'. 'Damisk vest and breeches wt ane pair stripped breeches'. The furred bedgown, worn with the flowered nightgown and the silk slippers must have made bedtime very fine. Tarbat also owned a wallet 'wt. comb case'.

He had copper-coloured stockings of silk, as well as two pairs of black silk stockings and several others. For his journeys he may have worn the 'hodden grey coat with vest of same' and 'the hair stuff cloack lined with red'. The 'Meikle coat with silver lacing' must have been for state occasions.

Eight years later an even fuller list of '*Clothes etc. belonging to the Earl of Cromartie at Whitehall was taken on 11 December 1704.*' There had been changes since the previous list. Tarbat had become an Earl, he had married again, and at this point was Her Majesty's Secretary of State for Scotland, and his deportment would have been correspondingly great. He evidently still had a taste for finery:

> A fine whit mixt-colored cloth suit, trimmed wt silver and a pr of stockings to the suit and a pr. of silver garters, A dark cloth cinnamon-coloured suit wit gold trimmings and a pair of stockings to the suit and a pair of gold garters.

The first must have been a shot-silk garment. There are several other suits, one of sky blue cloth, with coat, breeches and stockings. The Hodden grey coat is now 'Lyned with Todskins' [fox furs] and several other coats and waistcoats are fur-lined, some with squirrel. The swanskin for which the bill was paid along with my lady's sables has been made into 'a pair of swanskin foot socks'. There is an 'orang flour'd silver vest' and a new gray quilted silk nightgown. Right up-to-date new fashions were 'baver [beaver] hatts and a baver muff and a case for it'. The times were not always propitious for embroidered-waistcoated old gentlemen of seventy-three; also listed are '3 pairs of Pistols' and 'a little hangar [sword] with ane aggatt gripe and brass hilt'. Reflecting the fact that Cromartie was a keen member of the Royal Company of Archers of Scotland, and was their Captain for many years is the fact that he took 'A Bow and 12 arrow' to Whitehall.

Listed always with his clothes and shaving gear are:

> A littel tin pot for coffee or te
> a littel tin saucepan
> a Coffie roaster, and copper pot conforme ['conform' means matching]
> a copper boiler with a chimnie conform,
> a tinn lamp for oyle.
> two shaded brass candlesticks.

A strong impression comes over from this list of an elderly man who does not sleep well, but makes himself comfortable. The many journeys he must have undertaken between Edinburgh and London, by sea, and from Leith to his own ports in Ross, have not left much trace on the records. In

24   George, third Earl of Cromartie, his wife Countess Isabella and their eldest
surviving son, John Lord MacLeod, wearing Roman dress. Painted about 1741.

25 Lady Isabella, who looked after her parents in their banishment 'doing the most menial tasks'. She eventually inherited the Estate in 1799, when she was Lady Elibank.

his younger days he rode between Edinburgh and Dingwall; Brodie of Leithen records more than once giving dinner to Tarbat as he passed (it was when they were both in a joint undertaking to buy the Laird of Cromarty out of his old property). Later some of the Earl's travel must have been by ponderous coach, though the road south from Edinburgh was very foul, and at this time the coach-road north did not exist. He lists a lot of luggage:

> A large seath-skin trunk and a black leather French one
> A bent Leather portmantle and a pair leather baggs
> a red velvet and a pair velvet bags
> a pair of welvet baggs for papers
> a boarskin bag

In listing his papers later Cromartie notes that some were in the chest marked with a rose, which he draws, a formal Tudor rose; others were 'in the chist marked with a thrissle', and he draws a convincing thistle. As an officer of state he must always have travelled with a mass of important papers with him, in 'the welvet baggs'. He also had, as the fashion of the day demanded:

> A full bottom perwig and two knot chapineons.

These are listed again, but with the addition of their colours, the full bottom wig is 'pretty dark' and the two 'Champine Perwiggs' are 'both light colour'. There is also 'a half length wig of light hair and two short round-about wigs'.

For the clothes of the second and third Earls and their families we have to rely on portraits only. The fine portraits of John, as Master of Tarbat, and his first wife, show them most fetchingly dressed in orange silk with silver lacings and peach silk trimmings. They may have run up enormous bills with the tailor, Robert Blackwood, but they looked very fine. Blackwood's day of reckoning came, eventually.

The third Earl and his wife 'Bonnie Bel' were painted several times, most notably in a curious classical masquerade, with their eldest son John. The Earl wears greaves on his legs, and a vaguely toga-like garment. The boy carries a dove: the symbolism is lost. They were clearly proud of their family, whose pictures were painted several times. There is a painting of a curiously stiff little boy, William who died before he was ten, pictured in a cap and a long green coat like a dressing gown. In another painting the two elder girls and their brother John share a bowl of fruit. The eldest, Isabella, called after her mother, is alone in a half length picture of some charm, when aged about sixteen. It was this child who looked after her parents after the dark days in the Tower of London, doing the most menial tasks, as she after recalled.

The only other portrait of Isabella to survive was taken of her in old age, when she had inherited the estates as Lady Elibank, and is a mittened and well-set-up dowager. The military men, are all painted in full uniform, Lord John MacLeod by Romney, wearing his decorations from the King of Sweden as well as his uniform of King George. His brother Colonel George, who predeceased him, and his nephew Captain Kenneth who inherited, were painted half-length by an unknown but able painter, both uniformed. James Lord Royston was painted in his robes as a Lord of Session Judge.

The Library and Learning
of the First Earl

All through his life George, the first Earl, was a collector of good books, a taste he passed on to his son John, who was interested in good bindings and elegant editions.

As early as 1682 a London bookseller, James Fraser, a man who must have had his origin in the north, wrote a friendly letter to Lord Tarbat, gently reminding him that there was a small account for books outstanding for the past nine years, books from Paris, at the cost of £16. 17*s*. 0*d*. sterling. He said he hoped Lord Tarbat would also remember to send 'The Loch Fine or Loch Brine' herring which he had promised. In January 1692 he wrote again, a little more tersely, reiterating the outstanding book bill, and again asking for some more herring from Loch Fyne, which would be very handy for Lent. Fraser was a cultivated correspondent, giving news of international politics, and having connections with the French court. Almost certainly at this time that implied connections with the court of the exiled King James at Ste. Germaine, though the letters we have are too discreet to own the connection. Lovat, chief of Fraser, was to-and-fro at this time; much later his daughter published a justification for his political career and Jacobite sympathies, written in French.

After the first earl died, someone took an inventory of *The Earle of Cromartie's books at Castle Leod: taken 11 December 1714*. There are over a hundred titles, and many of them consist of several volumes. It is an interesting collection, a working library for a statesman; some law, some religious works, travel, and leisure reading as well. The categories merge and some of the books are hard to identify from the inventory's description; the taker was not a French speaker. Fifteen volumes of the *Théâtre de Corneille* rub shoulders with Dr Stillingsteel's *Sermons* and some (but not all) of the works of Horace. There are a number of travel books, some very up to date: Tavernier's *Les Six Voyages* (published in Paris in 1676) would have given, as they still do, an authentic contemporary view of the Court of the Great Moghul in India and the diamond mines of Golconda. Other traveller's tales were *The present state of Aegypt*—no author given— *Baiazet, Prince Othoman*: *Voyages de Siam*: *Historie de la religion des Turcs*

153

alongside *L'historire Mahometane*. These with others listed would have given an unusually comprehensive picture of the known world of the East.

There were a number of atlases, and these included Blaau's famous work, with the Scottish maps drawn by Timothy Pont. There were several dictionaries, *Le Grand Dictionaire ffrançois-latin Augmenté*, the *Marrow of the French Tongue*, *Le Dictionnaire Geographique* and a Latin *Dictionaium historicum Geographicum Poelitum*. There were law books, standard ones: *Justinian*, *Grotius*: *An Essay considering the power of the Magistrate*: and a wide ranging selection of religious books, from *Le Rosaire de la Très Heures* [*sic*] to *Sir Hugh Campbell on the Lords Praier*. *Traitte de la religion Chrettienne* was alongside *Thucydides* and a life of Cardinal Mazarin, as well as a dubious work called *Les Strategems D'amour, dédiee a Madam la Dutchesse Mazarin*. There are the conventional slightly pornographic works of the age, even going back to an earlier day—Plutarch's *Lives* and *Juvenal*— with the *Historical Account of the amours of the Emperor Morroca*: and the original edition of *Les Chroniques de Gargantua*, not the English translation by his father's old friend Sir Thomas Urquhart of Cromarty. Other titles are given inadequately or are doubtful. Probably the greatest number of books are French histories of great men or events—*Histoire de L'Eglise et de L'Empire, par Jean le Sueur*, or *La vie du Vicomte De Turenne* for example. There were Spanish copies of Cervantes: of *Il Cortigiano* [*the Courtier*] in Italian; books on Spanish America, in Spanish, and possibly the best thumbed of all, '*Machiavel*'. There are a few scientific works: *Rudimenta Geometrica*: *De Chemicorum cum Aristotelicis etc Galenius* (hardly up to date) and a work of less repute: *La Physique Occulette ou Traitte de la Baguelle Divinatoire*. There was also an *Acts of the General Assembly of the Church of Scotland*. There is only a couple of books which seem to refer to England: *A Consideration upon the Union of the Two Kingdoms*, and *Brittain or a Chronological description of the most flourishing kingdoms England, Scotland, Ireland and the Islands adjoining out of the depths of Antiquitie*. This title, lovingly transcribed in full by the maker of this list enables us to identify one book for sure: Camden's *Brittania* subtitled just as given, came out in a much enlarged edition of 1607. *The works of Benjamin Jonson* and *Hudibras* are the only works of the English imagination: no other great seventeenth century figure appears. One would hardly expect to find Milton or Marvell on the shelves of so ardent a cavalier, but one would have expected Shakespeare, even the early Swift, Dryden, or Pope. This is the library of one whose tastes were formed when he was young, in his thirties say, and living abroad.

The Earl kept up to date though, reading the newspapers and periodicals of the day, as they were sent to him by correspondents. Towards the end of his life James, his son, sent him in London 'The two last *Scots Tatlers*, they are prettie well done, for a Mac, I do not know the author, tho' most think it is Sir Arch, Sinclair'. Sad to note the Scottish inferiority complex so well developed so soon after the Union. His friend Professor Gregorie wrote from Oxford sending him the latest catalogue of 'our Press here'.

Although there are no Scottish writers on this list, Earl George betrayed his familiarity with at least Sir David Lindsay, when he quoted *Squire Meldrum* in a letter to a friend.

The most careful search among the books at Castle Leod today has not disclosed one book which can definitely be held to be one of those on Earl George's list. This is not surprising perhaps. The house was long let; troops were said to have been billeted there in 1746; Meddat used the great hall as a girnel to warehouse grain. It was left to Duchess Anne in mid-Victorian days to rehabilitate this lovely castle. And, even worse for the books, sometime between the time of the first Earl's death and the annexation of the estate, there are two letters to the surgeon-apothecary of Inverness asking for arsenic for the rats 'which are eating the old man's books'. Norman Macleod, that faithful barely literate chamberlain of the second Earl's, mentioned damage to books by damp as well as rats in the straitened days of the 1720s. As some of the bills of Fraser mention 'the Elizar editions' and 'the books of the Louvre printings', this loss is very sad. In view of the number of books on the East, the loss of the Japanned furniture and the pictures and tapestry described as Indian and Othoman in the Inventar of Royston and subsequent lists is tantalising. Earl George may have been, on this slender evidence, among the first in Scotland to feel that strange affinity with the East that so many Scots felt so strongly in the next century or more.

The first Earl published about twenty papers on political and historical topics. The titles are mostly listed by Sir William Fraser, though he omits one of the most important, *The History of the family of Mackenzie*, and he does not include the paper printed by Rev Robert Graham in his *Secret Commonwealth* in which Tarbat describes and assesses three examples of the Second Sight which lay within his experience. Graham was Minister of Aberfoyle in Perthshire, an episcopalian with the interests of his Gaelic congregation at heart: he translated the psalms into Erse, and sent for copies of the Erse Bible from Ireland, through his contacts with Tarbat and his friend Lord Boyle. *The Secret Commonwealth* is not exactly a political work, it categorises the ancient tribes of fairies as a serious work of anthropology.

The *History* had a long lasting influence on the concept of clan Mackenzie, through his painstaking and occasionally grandiose approach to family history. He is not accurate; in claiming distinguished ancestors for the Mackenzies Tarbat was enhancing his family as much as his building of New Tarbat and Royston had done. A modern genealogist David Sellar has devoted a whole article, *Highland Family Origins—Pedigree making and pedigree faking*, to an examination of the origins of the Mackenzies and other northern Highland families. Sellar takes them back to one Gilleoin of the Aird, and behind him to 'Cormach and his father Aibertach, who lived a century or so after Macbeth', and were Gaelic aristocrats of the tribe of Loarn. Lord Tarbat also takes the family back to Gilleoin, but transforms him into Colin Fitzgerald, a mythical younger son of a great Irish-Norman connection; the urge to find a Norman ancestor had reached the furthest north of Scotland. Tarbat knew enough to place a great deal of weight on the oral evidence of the Gaelic bards or sennachies, whom he equated with the Senators of classic Rome, and he knew a fair amount about the Picts and of High Irish history—or he claimed to. It was not so easy then to check on claims of learning made by distinguished old gentlemen, especially when their learning coincided with public expectation of nobility. What his long and detailed family history does demonstrate is the strength of the oral tradition in the Highlands translated into a written tradition by a learned son who had access to the spoken or sung records of the sennachies. Accuracy was not so important: the tradition of Praise Poems is strong in Gaelic literature. The seventeenth century was the threshold between the oral and literate traditions, as even *The Secret Commonwealth of Fairies* demonstrates.

Of Tarbat's other works, some refer to his chief political endeavour, the Union of Scottish and English parliaments. Four or five pamphlets, under the general heading of *Brief and Modest Reflexions*, deal with the position and doctrines of the Episcopal church in Scotland. One paper dealt with the currency and the silver shortage of 1695 in which some of his own plate had been swallowed by the Mint. He wrote a long *Historical account of the Conspiricies of the Earls of Gowrie* against the young King James VI of Scotland, which he hoped would please Queen Anne, James' great grand daughter. In his younger days he had written an *Account of Hirta and Rona*, which his old friend Sir Robert Sibbald preserved. Tarbat had visited the remote Isles when on the run from General Monck after the end of Glencairn's rising in 1656 or so; he also published works on meteorology, and on mosses, in the *Proceedings of the Royal Society* based on this voyage. He and Sir Robert Moray must have had ample opportunity for observing the weather and the variety of mosses while they avoided arrest in the Western Isles.

Tarbat's most lasting gift to scholarship and to Scotland, however, was in connection with the law. When he became Lord Clerk Register he became aware of the great damage to the records of Scotland done (he claimed) by invading Englishmen—King Edward I in the thirteenth century and Oliver Cromwell in his own day. Vital documents had been hidden and carried from one safe place to another, their exact whereabouts frequently forgotten. Tarbat was aware how incomplete they were, even those of his own day.

Tarbat created the Register of Saisins, in which every land transaction must and every civil one may be registered in Edinburgh for all time, by drawing up a copy. It is ironic that the present splendid Register House which contains them, was built by Robert Adam from the profits made by the Crown from the Forfeited and Annexed Estates in the second half of the eighteenth century. Cromartie's estate, so laboriously built up for his family, was one of the largest of those annexed, and returned after heavy payment in 1784.

An undated paper in the first Earl's hand (probably written about 1706), describes a most interesting project, one which sadly came to nothing. The paper is headed 'On Education' and begins with the rather trite aphorism 'That education in good literature is an excellent means to make mankind happy and wise no one will deny', and he goes on with a carefully worked-out proposal to build a proto-university in Inverness. Sensibly he begins with the funding of such an institution:

> Proposed that the stipends of the vacant kirks benorth the Spey for 21 years may (by act of this parliament) be destined and assigned to start and sustain three professors in the burgh of Inverness, one for Latin, Greek and Hebrew languages, one for Mathematics especially for arithmetic and geometry, and one for Morality ...

He goes on to suggest the probable money available from the vacant charges, (over 100 parishes in Ross and Inverness-shires) and the payment to be made to the professors, 'each salary so moch yearly', beginning with the Professor of Morality, 'so soon as the rent should amount to one salary; then to the Professor of Mathematics, ... and thridly to the Professor of Humanity'. Humanity evidently embraced the literature of the three languages he proposed should be studied. He made it clear he was not proposing to poach the pupils of 'The present grammar school which is to continue on its proper and present found'. When funds permitted the payment of a second professor, but not before, he was to be appointed. 'The salary to be for every Master 800 Merks besides a loging House'. He then envisages the setting, which if ever built, would have given Inverness a University enclosed in a courtyard in the manner of Old Glasgow College:

> That the township of Inverness build the said three lodging houses on their expenses and a common school room for each Professor, in some healthful convenient place, with a common garden to the three professors and a salary for one man to be housekeeper and gardener.

Moving on to the syllabus to be offered, the Earl proposed that 'those masters should teach publick lessons for one hour, two days in the week for each profession'—an early example of adult, or 'continuing' education? Even more in advance of his time he recommended that

> All men should be admitted to hear or learn mathematicks and humanity, and both men and women to hear morality (having distinct seats for each sexe) and that humanity be taught in the aforesaid three learned tongues, but morality and mathematics in the Scots language.

These high minded proposals are seen in a different light by the next proviso: 'That the young ones above seven years and below 16 years be examined in the afternoon, by their respective masters, each in his day'.

Both in the age of the students, and in the ambiguity about teaching in Latin or in the mother tongue, the Earl is in line with the conservative tradition of his own day. 'That no reward be taken by the Masters [from] particular persons, nor any besides their salaries', was perhaps a prudent stipulation. The paper ends with an elaborate outline of the administrative background of Inverness College, proposing a General Council elected from 'the nobility of every shire benorth the Spey and Burrows [Burghs] with two ministers out of every synod, changing every third year, and a Burgher from Inverness, Elgin, Forres, Dingwall, Tain, Fortrose and Dornoch.' A quorum of seven, and working council of 'those most often in Inverness' was proposed, and special meetings could be called at fourteen days notice. Nothing more is found in the papers about this liberal and far-sighted project. The reluctance of the presbyterians to commit the stipends of the vacant non-juring parishes to such a long term educational project, and a project with balanced kirk and town representation, probably was its ruin.

The End

The first Earl of Cromartie's hope
to the author, and to the Reader

'That I may leave something at length to somebody who may recall Laird of Tarbatt and who may perhaps recover as much out of that as my Grandfather and I did, out of loss. And, if not, God's will be done, for the warld was other folks' before us and will be after us. For who can now find the Heirs or Representatives of Allexd. [the Great], of Caesar, or of Socrides or Plato? But thanks be to God we are of a holy Religion which invites us to a glorious and everlasting Inheritance.'

Line of Mackenzie of Tarbat, Earls of Cromartie

Kintail Mackenzie

I Sir Roderick of Castle Leod,
Second son of Colin, Lord of Kintail
Coigach and Tarbat, Kt, Tutor of Kintail.
m. Margaret MacLeod, Heiress of Coigach
1606 died 1626

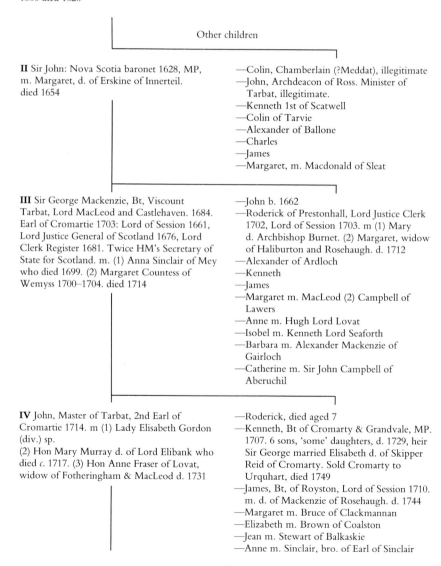

Other children

II Sir John: Nova Scotia baronet 1628, MP,
m. Margaret, d. of Erskine of Innerteil.
died 1654

—Colin, Chamberlain (?Meddat), illegitimate
—John, Archdeacon of Ross. Minister of
　Tarbat, illegitimate.
—Kenneth 1st of Scatwell
—Colin of Tarvie
—Alexander of Ballone
—Charles
—James
—Margaret, m. Macdonald of Sleat

III Sir George Mackenzie, Bt, Viscount
Tarbat, Lord MacLeod and Castlehaven. 1684.
Earl of Cromartie 1703: Lord of Session 1661,
Lord Justice General of Scotland 1676, Lord
Clerk Register 1681. Twice HM's Secretary of
State for Scotland. m. (1) Anna Sinclair of Mey
who died 1699. (2) Margaret Countess of
Wemyss 1700–1704. died 1714

—John b. 1662
—Roderick of Prestonhall, Lord Justice Clerk
　1702, Lord of Session 1703. m (1) Mary
　d. Archbishop Burnet. (2) Margaret, widow
　of Haliburton and Rosehaugh. d. 1712
—Alexander of Ardloch
—Kenneth
—James
—Margaret m. MacLeod (2) Campbell of
　Lawers
—Anne m. Hugh Lord Lovat
—Isobel m. Kenneth Lord Seaforth
—Barbara m. Alexander Mackenzie of
　Gairloch
—Catherine m. Sir John Campbell of
　Aberuchil

IV John, Master of Tarbat, 2nd Earl of
Cromartie 1714. m (1) Lady Elisabeth Gordon
(div.) sp.
(2) Hon Mary Murray d. of Lord Elibank who
died *c.* 1717. (3) Hon Anne Fraser of Lovat,
widow of Fotheringham & MacLeod d. 1731

—Roderick, died aged 7
—Kenneth, Bt of Cromarty & Grandvale, MP.
　1707. 6 sons, 'some' daughters, d. 1729, heir
　Sir George married Elisabeth d. of Skipper
　Reid of Cromarty. Sold Cromarty to
　Urquhart, died 1749
—James, Bt, of Royston, Lord of Session 1710.
　m. d. of Mackenzie of Rosehaugh. d. 1744
—Margaret m. Bruce of Clackmannan
—Elizabeth m. Brown of Coalston
—Jean m. Stewart of Balkaskie
—Anne m. Sinclair, bro. of Earl of Sinclair

V George, 3rd Earl of Cromartie. m. Isabella d. of Sir William Gordon of Invergordon, Kt, & 1st Bart. Out for Prince Charles Edward 1745–46. Estate forfeited and titles attainted. d. London 1766.

VII Capt Roderick. Royal Dragoons whose son Capt Kenneth succeeded to uncle in estates, 1789. d. 1796
—William (army career)
—Patrick or Peter, Merchant in Jamaica
—Gideon died of small pox 1714
—Helen
(3rd wife)
—Norman (Army)
—Hugh (Army)
—Mary dsp 1726
—Anne dsp
—Amelia m. Lamont

VI John Lord Macleod and Count of Sweden, Col of Macleod's Highlanders attainted but pardoned for part in Rising. b. 1727 m. Marjory d. of Lord Forbes no issue. Recovered Cromartie Estates 1784, died 1789

VIII Isabella b. 1726 m. Lord Elibank 1760 & succeeded cousin Kenneth as eighth in line of estates 1796. died 1801. Succeeded by daughter
IX Maria Hay Mackenzie through whom the present line descends.
—William, died aged 7
—George, Lt Col of 71st Foot Lord MacLeod's Highlanders, died in Madras 1787
—Mary married in America (1) Capt Clarke 1750; (2) Mr Drayton, Councillor, S. Carolina; (3) John Ainslie Esq
—Anne (1) Hon Edmond Atkin; (2) Dr Murray
—Caroline (1) Mr Drake; (2) Walter Hunter of Polmood
—Jane dsp. in Edinburgh about 1821
—Amelia died of smallpox aged 7
—Margaret (Peggie) m. John Glasford of Dougalston, Glasgow
—Augusta m. Sir Wm Murray

Tables of Measure

Currency

Scots	Sterling
1 penny	1/12th penny (quarter farthing)
1 shilling	1 penny
13 shillings, 4 pence = 1 Merk	$1s.1\frac{1}{2}d.$
20 shillings, one pound Scots	$1s. 8d.$
Twelve pounds Scots	one pound sterling

Capacity = liquid measure according to the Jugg of Stirling, 1661.

Scots	Imperial	metric
1 gill	0.749 gill	0.053 litre
4 gills = 1 mutchkin	2.996 gill	0.212 ,,
2 mutchkin = 1 chopin	1 pint	0.848 ,,
2 chopin = 1 pint	2 pints 3.9 gill	1.696 ,,
8 pints = 1 gallon	3 gallons 0.25 gill	13.636 ,,

Dry Measure according to the Boll of Linlithgow, 1661

used for measurements of barley, oats and malt. The Great Boll of Tarbat was considerably larger.

1 lippie			3.037 litres
4 lippies = 1 peck		1 peck	13.229 litres
4 pecks = 1 firlot	1 bushel	1 peck	52.916 litres
4 firlots = 1 boll	5 bushel	3 peck	211.664 litres
16 bolls = 1 chalder	11 quarters	5 bushel	3386.624 litres

Linear Measure

1 inch	1.0016 inches	2.54 centimetres
12 inches = 1 foot	12.0192 ,,	22.55 ,,
$3^1/_{12}$ feet = 1 ell	37.0598 ,,	94.1318 ,,
1 mile	1.123 miles	1.8073 kilometre

Based on *The Concise Scots Dictionary*, Aberdeen 1985

Glossary

anent concerning, about.

anker small cask holding about a quart liquid measure.

aquavitie water of life, whisky, usqubae.

ashet, asset a serving plate, usually oval; a pie dish.

barill barrel.

barm yeast.

Baron Baillie (court) Legal law court held by the Baron, or his representative, the Depute, to hear local cases.

baver beaver, beaver-skin hat.

beasts cattle, usually when in a drove.

bere, bear, beer barley a commonly grown form of barley, four-horned.

bern bairn, young child.

birken, birken railes rails made of birch wood.

boll see table of quantities, a grain measure.

botell bottle.

brint burnt.

burden load of a ship, tonnage estimate.

Burgess citizen of a Burgh, a merchant of a guild.

caisson small chest; cp cassone (It.).

cannol cinnamon.

caplagan (spellings various, e.g. capligain) The perquisites of a ship's captain, usually a barrel of ale and a boll of oatmeal (normal in the late 17th century Bills of Lading).

carl serving man, a peasant.

cassy-chrom West Highland foot-plough (cas-chrom, Gaelic).

cautioner One who stands surety: a guarantor.

chaffer a portable stove.

chalder see table of quantities: a grain measure.

chamberlain the chief executive servant of a large landowner, later called the Factor.

champine, champinon a full wig.

chin-cough whooping cough.

clogback a trunk with a domed lid, *or* a saddle-bag, sometimes cloak-bag.

cock o'leekie a favourite old soup made from stewed hens and leeks, with the addition of prunes.

cog, cogg a wooden pail or deep bowl, for milking, or other liquids.

conform matching.

creel a deep basket, especially for carrying peats on the back.

curran currant, dried currant.

damisk damask, figured linen fabric.

dight to winnow grain, to make grain clean and ready for sale.

distrenzie distrain, to compel the sale of goods to satisfy a creditor, take goods in lieu of legal dues.

dizen dozen.

doer factotum: usually a legal but humble rôle: to do or execute the lord's business.

eboyne ebony wood.

ell Scots yard.

fatt vat, vessel.

ferret ferret fur, i.e. ermine.

Feu feudal tenure of land.

Fiars' fixed (nominal) price of grain, adjusted annually by local government to assist calculations between grain and money rents, especially in the stipend of a Minister.

filamort perhaps from féileadh-mòr, 'philamor' or Highland dress: see *plaid*: possibly a suit of jacket and breeches made from plaiding.

finear, fineared veneer, veneered.

firlot see table of quantities.

flannin flannel.

flesher butcher.

fourgett small kitchen measure.

fryed (of fabric) frayed.

furd furred.

gad measure of pig-iron.

garron Scots pony, a sturdy small horse.

gavel gable.

gird baking sheet or girdle.

girnel, girnel house grain store, grain warehouse.

glasser glazier.

got tender pregnant.

gowen (1) daisy (2) gown.

gravat cravat or neck-cloth.

grieve farm bailiff.

grosset gooseberry.

gubenor governor or tutor, especially of small boys.

haill to haul up, as in a child learning to stand.

hair-stuff fabric woven with a proportion of horse-hair.

hangar a small sword.

harling rough-cast finish on masonry, mixture of lime, gravel and sand.

heritor property-owner or renter who has concomitant responsibility for public taxes, especially in connection with the parish.

Hodden-grey coarse undyed woollen fabric, natural coloured.

hogshead barrel: see tables.

holland fine strong linen, orig. from Holland.

imbroder embroider.

impost (1) signature (2) imposition.

indigor indigo dye, vegetable dye—cake imported from West Indies and later from India to give the darkest blue.

Insight plenishings inside furnishings.

Inventar inventory.

jeast joist, of roofing.

justicar a sleeved waistcoat (Fr. *just-au-corps*).

kaim or *kane* a rent payment in kind, e.g. hens, wedders, white plaids.

keai jackdaw.

kned knead.

knoope an ornamental fabric knob, usually tasseled.

lading loading, cargo.

last measure of barrels of fish: 12 barrels to one last.

leaven flour or meal and water, mixed with yeast, to rise.

leet measure of peat, here a stack 6 feet high, 12 feet square.

lippie see table: grain measure.

mantua a woman's loose/full gown, usually silk.

mealer a small tenant farmer, a cottar.

meikle large, great.

Mentieth large bowl for punch, or a small cistern on a wall, for drinking water.

merk Scots unit of currency, becoming obsolete in the 17th century: see tables of measure.

muchkin see table of measures.

nolt cattle.

padusoy silk of Padua.

paragon fine fabric, often fringed.

patronage the granting of a favour: the right of presentation of a Minister to a particular parish.

peck see tables of measure.

perjink trim, neat and straight laced.

perk perquisite.

pernickety precise, obsessed with detail, fussy.

pernickitie obsessed by detail, fussy.

Perwig periwig.

plaid rectangular length of cloth, us. 12 ft × 4 ft, worn belted to form a man's kilt, or a woman's shawl, or as a blanket. Twill weave, either tartan or the finer plain white.

pleached (sometimes *plet*) trees trained and intertwined in a regular manner, 'plaited' together and so pruned. Gardens only.

plenishing furnishing, equipment.

poind to seize or impound the goods of a debtor.

pokker poker, fire-irons.

policy, policies the surrounding park of a mansion house.

popish, papish pertaining to the Pope of Rome.

porringer porage bowl.

portmantle suitcase.

precept written authorisation.

press cupboard.

pultess poultice, dressing of a wound.

pynor a lowly general labourer.

quarrier stone-mason.

quincunx orchard planting in lines of five, to appear straight from diagonal corners as well as from sides: as in "5" on dice.

raused a stage in the process of winnowing bere barley from the ear: prob. from meaning to beat or thrash, and possibly to riddle through a sieve.

remit referral of a matter to a higher authority: or the authority itself.

roup auction sale.

ruad rood, see table.

sabel sable fur.

sahel, saugh willow.

samen same, similar.

sark (1) planking for a roof on which slates are nailed (2) sacking.

scallag a farm labourer, a boy.

scattin satin.

selak sealskin leather trunk perhaps from 'selkie' a seal.

serbin serving, servant.

shalloune edging, border decoration.

shirrifdom Sheriff's jurisdiction.

shizors scissors.

shoffel shovel.

skaith damage, injury.

skimpy short measure, barely adequate.

skreen screen.

sled a sledge.

sled sledge, for farm uses.

slighted deliberate ruination of a fortification, to render it useless for warfare.

sonsy good-looking.

steading farmyard.

tabelroom dining room.

Tack (1) a lease of land from a principal landowner; the paper on which the Rental Contract was written. (2) a sixpence, lowland usage.

Tacksman holder of a big lease, usually the kinsman of the main landholder, esp. in Mackenzie circles.

Talidores a kind of picture.

teynd, teind tithe or tenth part of rental due to the church.

thrissle thistle.

tocher daughters' dowry.

Todskins fox furs.

Tour de loos the bunches of feathers, usually ostrich, ornamentally used at the four corners of a state four-poster bed.

trams cart shafts, or machinery in general.

twillet twilled weave of fabric.

tyke mongrel dog, so, a tousled rough person.

wadset form of land mortgage, a loan from tenant to landowner. If not redeemed the tenant gains the land.

wagery wages, dues.

wanscot wainscot, applied either to pannelled rooms, or to cabinet-made furniture.

wark (building) work.

wedder castrated male lamb (paid as rent).

whey buttermilk.

whin gorse.

whit white.

widd wide.

winning (of stones, etc.) quarrying.

woll wool.

worstet worsted woollen cloth.

wright skilled workman; a squarewright was a joiner.

Writer to the Signet: senior solicitors appearing in the High Court of Sessions, Edinburgh. (W.S.).

Index